Buffi Duberman

100 WAYS TO SAVE YOUR A$$ IN ENGLISH

100 MANIEREN OM JE ENGELS TE VERBETEREN VOOR ELKE BUSINESS SITUATIE

B

EERSTE DRUK

© 2016 BUFFI DUBERMAN
www.buffiduberman.com

Ontwerp en vormgeving: Peter Kortleve, Shortlife Graphic Design
Foto omslag: Ringel Goslinga
Drukkerij: Wilco

ISBN: 978 90 821301 1 9
NUR: 632

Niets uit deze uitgave mag worden verveelvoudigd, opgeslagen in een geautomatiseerd gegevensbestand, of openbaar gemaakt, in enige vorm of op enige wijze, hetzij elektronisch, mechanisch, door fotokopieën, opnamen of op enige manier, zonder voorafgaande schriftelijke toestemming van de auteur.

Teksten zijn gezet in Futura, Bebas Neue, Eastside Texture en Andada.

DEDICATION

FOR YOU, DEAR READER,
AND YOUR SOON-TO-BE-SAVED ASS.

By buying this book, you have helped, not only yourself, but also someone else.
A portion of the proceeds generated from the sale of this book will
be used to fund educational materials for refugees in the Netherlands.
I cannot thank you enough for your support.

TABLE OF CONTENTS

Voorwoord: Taal is alles, *door Jan Marijnissen* — 12

Introduction: Are you ready? — 14

Section One
THE 30 MOST EMBARRASSING ENGLISH MISTAKES
And How Not To Make Them

CHAPTER 1
COMMUNICATION CONFUSION

01. 'My Name's Gerard. That's J-I-R-E-R-D.' — 18
The English Alphabet, and A vs. An

02. 'Ten Over Half What?!' — 22
Telling Time in English and Time-related Expressions

03. 'Time Is On Your Side. Yes It Is.' — 24
In Time vs. On Time

04. 'I Love It! Just Don't Bring Me Any...' — 26
Do vs. Would, and Formal Requests

05. 'Never Lie To Your Doctor!' — 28
Prepositions of Place and Time

06. 'Thanks For Sharing.' — 30
Long vs. Tall, and How to Organize Your New Words

07. 'This Is A Nightmare...' — 31
This Night vs. Last Night and Will vs. Going To

08. 'Remind Me To Remind You To Remember...Something?' — 33
Remind vs. Remember

09. 'I Have 99 Problems, And *Much* And *Many* Are Two of Them.'   34
    Much vs. Many vs. a Little vs. a Few

10. 'Make A To-do List...'   36
    Make vs. Do And Related Phrases

11. 'I'm Getting Used to The Fact That I Can Never Get Used To That.'   38
    Used To Doing vs. Used To Do And Related Expressions

12. 'Might Be More Interesting If You Turn It On First...'   40
    Look vs. Watch vs. See

13. 'Nice Ass!'   42
    Everything You Wanted To Know But Were Afraid To Ask

Don't Go There!   44
    Things You Should Never Say Again

CHAPTER 2
HAND AND MOUTH IMPROVEMENT

Pronunciation Predicaments   47

14. 'Ice Ice Baby.'   47
    The S vs. the Z Sound

15. 'Didn't I See That in *The Wizard of Oz*?'   50
    The TH Sound

16. 'From Buffi Wit Lof'   52
    The V vs. the F Sound

Writing Washouts

17. 'Don't Talk Like Yoda.'   52
    English Word Order

18. 'It Takes Two...Too...To Tango.'   58
    To, Too, Two, and Other Homonyms

19. 'Look Out!'   60
    Look Forward to And Prepositional Objects

20. 'If You Want to Sound Like A Cool Alien, Keep Doing This.'   62
Starting And Ending Emails And Letters

Spell Check Yourself Before You Wreck Yourself   64

Don't Go There!   67

CHAPTER 3
GRAMMAR GRIEF

21. 'No Horsehead in the Bed, I Beg of You!'   70
The Present Tenses

22. 'Now You...Know.'   73
Past Simple Tense and Regular vs. Irregular Verbs

23. 'BAD GRAMMAR CAN KILL!'   76
Present Perfect and Past Continuous Tenses

24. 'Take Me to Vegas, Baby!'   77
If vs. When and Conditionals, Types 1, 2, and 3

25. 'Are You Spiderman?'   81
Prepositions of Place

26. 'You Need Me. More Than You Think!'   83
Good vs. Well and Adjectives vs. Adverbs

27. 'Hardly Working? Aha...So How Was *Extreme Couponing Makeovers With The Stars...On Ice?*'   86
Hard vs. Hardly and Comparison of Adjectives

28. 'Do This if You Want to Start a Fight.'   88
Question Tags and Possessive Pronouns

29. 'It's All in the Wrist!'   91
Reflexive Verbs

30. 'How to Give Me A Heart Attack.'   92
Phrasal Verbs

Don't Go There!   95

Section Two
LET'S GET DOWN TO BUSINESS, YO
How To Rock Your English In Any Business Situation

CHAPTER 4
LET'S PUT THE 'PRESENT' BACK IN PRESENTATIONS

31. How to Triple Your Vocabulary Fast	100
(And Make The Right Connection)	
32. Kill Those Nerves And B-R-E-A-T-H-E	101
33. Know Your Audience (And Get Sushi)	102
34. Know Your Purpose	102
35. Know Your Shizzle	103
36. Introduction to Awesomeness	103
37. The Wow Factor	104
38. A Totally Terrific Template	105
39. Let's Get Connected!	107
40. Dealing With Questions	108
41. It's All About The Nipples	109
42. The Third Eye	109

CHAPTER 5
GETTING THE 'GO' IN NEGOTIATIONS

43. A Warm Welcome	111
44. Terms and Conditionals	112
45. Conditionals Type 1: The Promise	112
46. Conditionals Type 2: When Doubt Enters The Room	113

47. Looking Back	114
48. Don't Make An Ass Out Of U And Me	115
49. My Recipe For A Bad News Sandwich	116
50. A Compromising Situation	117

CHAPTER 6
AGREEING, DISAGREEING, AND ASKING WHAT THEY THINK

51. Hell, Yeah	118
How To Agree Completely, Totally, And Wholeheartedly	
52. Definitely Maybe	119
How To Partially Agree	
53. No Way, José	120
Absolute And Total Disagreement	
54. So Close…And Yet So Far	121
Expressing Partial Disagreement	
55. Hit Me Baby One More Time	121
Using Time Indications To Leave The Door Open	
56. R-E-S-P-E-C-T	122
Find Out What It Means To Them	
57. Tell Me What You Want	122
What You Really, Really Want	

CHAPTER 7
I KNOW WHEN THAT HOTLINE BLINGS, IT CAN ONLY MEAN ONE THING

58. 'Hello, It's Me'	124
Introducing Yourself	
59. 'Who You Gonna Call?'	125
Asking For Someone	

60. Ice, Ice, Baby 125
And How To Break It

61. Tell Me Why (You Are Calling) 126

62. Tonight's The Night 127
Setting Up a Meeting

63. Sorry Seems To Be The Hardest Word 127
How To Change Or Cancel An Appointment Without Pissing Them Off

64. 'No, You Hang Up First!' 129
Saying Goodbye

65. Pick Up Line 129
How to Answer the Phone

66. Is It Me You're Looking For? 130
Finding Out More

67. You're Breaking Up 131
What To Say When You Have A Bad Connection

68. You Got Me Hanging On The Telephone: 131
How To Take Messages

CHAPTER 8

LIKE A BOSS: NETWORKING LIKE A NATIVE

69. Good Old Times 133

70. Say My Name, Say My Name 134
How To Introduce Yourself To New People

71. Tell Me More 135
Finding Out More About What Someone Does (And Why!)

72. Introducing Someone Else 135

73. Welcome To My World 135
What To Say When You Forgot Someone's Name.

74. I'll Tell You All About It When I See You Again: How To Keep In Touch 136

CHAPTER 9
PASSPORT PROOF: ENGLISH FOR (BUSINESS) TRAVEL

75. Come Fly Away With Me — 137

76. Hot Wheels — 139

77. Room Service, Please — 145

78. Bite Me! — 145

79. Prada or Nada, Baby! — 148

CHAPTER 10
WHEN THE SHIT HITS THE FAN

80. Is There A Doctor in the House? — 150

81. Discussing Symptoms: Different Ways to Kvetch (Google it!) About Your Problems — 151

82. Let's Get Medicated — 152

83. You Look So Sick! — 153

84. To Catch A Thief — 153

85. At the Police Station — 154

86. Describing the Asshole Who Did It — 154

87. You Will Get Over This, I Promise You — 155

CHAPTER 11
ONE LANGUAGE DIVIDED BY A LOT OF WATER: THE BASIC DIFFERENCES BETWEEN BRITISH AND AMERICAN ENGLISH

88. Basic Spelling Differences — 157

89. Basic Grammar Differences — 157

90. Basic Vocabulary Differences — 157

CHAPTER 12
SPICE UP YOUR LIFE (AND MINE): 100 IDIOMS TO MAKE YOUR LIFE MORE EXCITING

91. Show Me The Money — 159

92. Let's Talk About Marketing And Sales — 160

93. What's Your Number? — 161

94. Tell Me About Success And Failure — 162

95. Efficiency Proficiency — 163

96. Color Your World — 164

97. Food Glorious Food — 165

98. Make Friends With Animals — 166

99. Where It's At — 167

100. He Shoots, He Scores — 168

ACKNOWLEDGMENTS

An Attitude Of Gratitude — 170

VOORWOORD

TAAL IS ALLES

We dromen in taal, we denken in taal, we werken samen met behulp van taal; de mens is taal. Zonder taal geen wetenschap, geen kennis, geen emotie; geen leven. Dat geldt wanneer je je uitdrukt in je moedertaal, maar komt nog dwingender tot uiting wanneer je je in een vreemde taal moet uitdrukken. En omdat het kleine Nederland wel erg veel buitenland heeft, is het spreken van de belangrijkste wereldtaal, het Engels, noodzakelijk wanneer je je over de landsgrenzen begeeft.

Het was 1993. Als leider van de SP was ik uitgenodigd op de eerste legale conferentie van het ANC in Johannesburg. Omdat mijn Engels nooit het middelbare schoolniveau was ontstegen (omdat ik er simpelweg niets mee gedaan had), besloot ik me te laten bijspijkeren. Ik ging één week naar de 'nonnen van Vught'. Ik heb in die week geen non gezien maar wel vier ontzettend leuke vrouwen: een Schotse, een Engelse, een Ierse en een Amerikaanse. De laatste, Buffi Duberman, de auteur van dit boek, was de allerleukste. We spraken over van alles: over onze landen, onze interesses, onze belangstelling voor muziek, maatschappij en politiek. Zo hoorde ik dat Buffi een bijzondere belangstelling heeft voor de Oostenrijks-Britse filosoof Ludwig Wittgenstein. Ze vertelde ook dat ze in haar jeugd heel veel dagen heeft doorgebracht in het Metropolitan Museum in haar toenmalige woonplaats, New York. Buffi is een bijzondere vrouw: ik leerde haar kennen als een uitstekende docent, erudiet en belangstellend, vol empathie. De gesprekken gingen vanaf dag één allemaal in het Engels. Want dat is immers de beste en snelste manier om een taal te leren. Doen!

Bij mijn bezoek aan Zuid-Afrika heb ik enorm veel profijt gehad van de opfriscursus bij Regina Coeli, trouwens ook bij de studiereis die ik in datzelfde jaar maakte naar de VS, en later naar onder andere Israël en Brazilië. Het (redelijk) beheersen van een taal geeft je het zelfvertrouwen om te zeggen wat gezegd moet worden en te vragen wat je graag weten wilt.

'Verdomd, ze is het!', riep ik uit. Iemand had mij geattendeerd op een leuk geklede vrouw die als coach optrad bij een songcontest op tv. Het was Buffi! Ze werkte inmiddels op de Rockacademie in Tilburg en begeleidde daar artiesten in spe bij het leren van de Engelse taal. We herstelden na bijna vijftien jaar het contact. Dat gaf mij de mogelijkheid om een brief die ik als (fractie)voorzitter van de SP aan de net aangetreden Amerikaanse president Obama wilde sturen door Buffi te laten vertalen; een brief aan de president van het belangrijkste land ter wereld moet natuurlijk foutloos zijn. Ik heb helaas zijn antwoord nooit mogen ontvangen...

In het najaar ga ik in Canada onderzoeken waarom dat land – hoewel gelegen in de Amerikaanse hemisphere – toch zoveel Europese trekken heeft. In velerlei opzicht wijkt het land af van de manier waarop in de VS de samenleving is ingericht. Ik hoop er dingen op te steken die bruikbaar zijn voor de Nederlandse verhoudingen. Met dank aan Buffi!

Jan Marijnissen

INTRODUCTION

ARE YOU READY?

Hello, gorgeous. Yes, I mean YOU. Thanks for holding me in your hands. I really like it here. I made this book just for you. Why? I decided to create this book after getting such positive reactions to my last book, *30 Ways to Save Your Ass in English*. However, this time I wanted to take it a (big) step further, and create a new platform for all my tips and tricks on raising the bar on professional communication in English. Thirty ways just wasn't enough anymore – I wanted to find even more ways of saving your ass in English.

As a professional corporate English coach and trainer, and an official TEDx speaker coach, I wanted to share my years of experience in the professional sector, and to let you know what really works based on the results I have seen firsthand with my clients. I have developed the second part of the book, with the fun(ky) title 'Let's Get Down To Business, Yo', to meet their needs. 'Let's Get Down To Business, Yo' is divided into different sections. Each subsection has a clear purpose and lots of handy phrases that will help you feel more confident, comfortable, and natural when it comes to professional business situations – whether they be presentations, meetings, vocabulary development, travel, or networking in English. I've also included 100 fabulous idioms to make your English sparkle, and explained the difference between American and British English. There's even a section called 'When The Shit Hits The Fan' to help you through a medical or legal crisis in English. I just want you to be safe and happy. And have awesome English skills, too!

I hope this book makes a difference in how you feel when you communicate in English. I loved writing this book. Well, most of the time. Sometimes I wanted to lick broken glass instead of writing, but still. You and your English needs are worth suffering for. That's how much I love you.

Now let the ass-saving begin.

Buffi Duberman

APRIL, 2016

Section One

SECTION ONE

THE 30 MOST EMBARRASSING MISTAKES IN ENGLISH
And How Not To Make Them

Well, darling, let's get started! The first part of this book deals with the 30 most embarrassing mistakes in English and how not to make them. I have heard every single mistake firsthand (hey, don't shoot the messenger!). Although it's fun to laugh about them, as a teacher, I really want you to *learn* from them. I explain why the mistake was made and how to correct it, so that you never have to look at surprised or shocked faces again.

There are three subsections here: Communication Confusion, Hand And Mouth Improvement, and Grammar Grief. Now, let's take the first step together in our ass-saving journey.

CHAPTER 1

COMMUNICATION CONFUSION

Our first section covers some of the basic mistakes people make when communicating in English. Many times you don't realize you've made a mistake until you see the surprised or confused faces of the people you've been talking to. Has this happened to you, my love? If so, you'll find out soon how to never go there again, and a smile will return to your gorgeous face very soon.

Section 1 covers lots of fun things — from telling time to the alphabet, from formal to informal language, prepositions, plurals, and more! We start with the basics and then kick it up a notch. Everyone has to know how to spell his or her name and tell time in English, but that's not as easy as you think. I've also got some handy phrases coming up soon, so make sure you have a notebook or a highlighter ready so that you can remember them easily! Ready? Ready.
Let's go.

01. "MY NAME'S GERARD. THAT'S J-I-R-E-R-D"

PROBLEM:
Gerard is not spelled 'J-i-r-e-r-d', but, obviously, 'G-e-r-a-r-d'.

DIAGNOSIS:
This person (and I suspect he's not the only one) has trouble saying the letters of the English alphabet correctly. He said J instead of G, I instead of E, and E instead of A. (The other letters were OK, thank God!) I know exactly where this problem stems from — the E in English is pronounced the same as the I in Dutch, the E in Dutch is the A in English, the I in English is the IJ in Dutch, and the I in Dutch is the E in English. No wonder we (by this I mean "you") get confused! Let me save your ass on this one.

REMEDY:

There is nothing more embarrassing than not being able to spell your own name. Can you imagine having a great phone call with a potential client and then asking them to send you an email confirming what you've just discussed, only to sound like a two-year-old when it comes to spelling your name in English? We don't want to go there, now, do we, darling?

This little trick will help you remember the most difficult letters in the English alphabet. (And no, we don't call this a 'donkey bridge' in English! It's a 'memory aid', or, if you really want to sound sexy, a 'mnemonic device'...but for some reason 'donkey bridge' sounds like more fun!) When you think of these letters, try to remember the following words:

A = LA, DNA
I = FBI, iPhone, iPad
E = email (ever heard of anyone wanting to check their amail?!)
U = university, United States
Y = YMCA, DIY, why (when you think of the Y, try to imagine the letter being formed by a person standing up with their arms in the air, wondering why. This works for me, but maybe only for me...)
G = Bee Gees, G-Star, G-Unit
J = DJ, JFK
K = OK
H = If you are a fashionista and have shopped abroad, then think of H&M. Otherwise, just memorize it – it sounds like the word *age*, but ends with a *tsh* sound – *aitsh*.

Extra Vitamins!

If you want to be able to spell with confidence (and you do! You do!), the best way is to practice with a friend. Spell for them the name of the street you live on, your mother's last name, the name of the school you went to, etc. Have them write down exactly what you said. Then read what they wrote and check how well you did! (Then switch to get revenge.)

If you use English on the phone a lot, it might be a good idea to copy my letter list, laminate it and place it next to your phone. Many of my clients have done this over the years, and made copies for all their colleagues. It works! Now, if we could just find Gerard to let him know...

> Je hoeft echt niet het hele *military alphabet* (Alpha, Bravo, Charlie, etc.) uit je hoofd te leren wanneer je woorden wilt leren spellen. Probeer dit lijstje eens! Kopieer het en hang het in de buurt van je telefoon.
>
> *A* als in apple
> *B* als in boy
> *C* als in car
> *D* als in dog
> *E* als in ear
> *F* als in flag
> *G* als in great
> *H* als in house
> *I* als in insect
> *J* als in joy
> *K* als in kind
> *L* als in light
> *M* als in magic
>
> *N* als in night
> *O* als in orchestra
> *P* als in people
> *Q* als in question
> *R* als in red
> *S*als in super
> *T* als in truck
> *U* als in unique
> *V* als in video
> *W* als in wow
> *X* als in xerox
> *Y* als in yes
> *Z* als in zebra
>
> In de VS wordt de z uitgesproken als het Nederlandse *zie*, en in het Brits spreken ze de z uit als *zed*.

Now that we've covered the letters of the alphabet, let's talk about how to use two letters in particular: the *a* and the *n*. A common problem in English is when to use *a* and when to use *an*. It's quite simple, really. It all depends on whether the first letter of the following word starts with a *vowel* (klinker) or a *consonant* (medeklinker). 'Say what, mama?' A vowel is *a, e, i, o,* or *u**, a consonant is *b, c, d,* etc.

If your word starts with a *vowel*, use *an*:
- an apple
- an elephant
- an interesting question
- an ordinary Sunday morning
- an understanding*

If your word starts with a *consonant*, use *a*:
- a banana
- a cat
- a dog
- a friendly policeman
- a garrulous person (Just thought I'd throw that one in there – *garrulous* means 'excessively talkative' or 'chatty'.)
- a university*

* LET OP!

Wanneer je een woord begint met een *u* kan het twee kanten op, afhankelijk van de klank van de *u*. Wanneer de *u* uitgesproken wordt als het Engelse woord *you*, gebruik je *a*:
- a university
- a universal truth
- a united front

Wanneer het woord begint met een *u* die wordt uitgesproken als uh, komt er *an* voor het woord:
- an undershirt
- an umbrella
- an unusual situation

02. 'TEN OVER HALF WHAT?!'

PROBLEM:
'I will see you at ten over half four.'

DIAGNOSIS:
This person was trying to say 'I will see you at 3.40.' This person failed.

REMEDY:
Telling time in English is pretty simple. (As opposed to telling time in Dutch. At least for me. That's why I never leave the house.) If the time you are talking about is precisely on the hour, then it's *o'clock*. 'The shops open at 9 o'clock.'

You can also say 'four o'clock sharp' or 'four o'clock on the dot' as other options (and if you want to sound snazzy). Fifteen minutes past the hour can be either 'a quarter past' or 'a quarter after', and 15 minutes before the hour is 'a quarter to'. Half past the hour is just that: 'half past four'.

> In Brits Engels hoor je vaak 'half six', 'half seven', 'half eight', etc. Dit zou je wel eens in verwarring kunnen brengen, want in tegenstelling tot het Nederlands betekent dit niet een half uur vóór het hele uur, maar een half uur ná het hele uur. Dus 'half six' betekent half zeven, 'half seven' half acht, etc. In Brits Engels wordt het woord 'past' dus weggelaten! (The first time I heard a British person say 'half six', I thought they meant 'three o'clock'.)

And for other times, we just say '5 past/after/to', '10 past/after/to' or '20 past/after/to', etc. Easy, right?

We always use the preposition 'at' to talk about times on the clock. But did you know that we also use it to talk about mealtimes?
'I will see you at dinner later this evening.'
'She met such a great guy at dinner that they ended up having breakfast together too.'

Extra vitamins!

Do you know the difference between A.M. and P.M.? In English, A.M. starts at midnight (00.00) and continues until noon (12.00). If you say, 'I was out until 2 in the night' that's wrong, because you were out, in English, until 2 in the morning. Which sounds like you partied much harder! P.M. is from noon until midnight. Although these words have Latin origins and actually stand for 'ante meridian' and 'post meridian', you can remember them easily by thinking of A.M. as after midnight, and P.M. as pre-midnight.

'AT NIGHT' OF 'IN THE NIGHT'?

We gebruiken 'at night' wanneer we het hebben over nachten **in het algemeen**:
'I'm used to living in the countryside, where it gets very dark at night.'
'He's a night nurse, so he sleeps during the day and works at night.'
'You need to remember to lock all of your doors before you go out at night.'

'In the night' wordt gebruikt wanneer je refereert aan een **specifiek moment** of een korte tijd gedurende de nacht:
'He woke up several times in the night because he heard strange noises outside.'
'She got up and got herself something to drink in the night because she was thirsty.'
'He remembered just how spicy his burritos were on several occasions in the night.'

And since we're on the subject of time, how about my top 10 English expressions using the word *time*? I say, 'Oooh, yes! Bring it!'

Quality time – spending time with people you love, doing something that you love:
'We need to spend more quality time with our families...eating chocolate.'

No time like the present – don't put off till tomorrow what you can do today:
'You'd like to join a gym? There's no time like the present! I'll drive you over!'

Time will tell – time will reveal the truth eventually:
'Time will tell if he's telling the truth – we just have to wait to get the test results back.'

Third time's a charm – this should work because it's the third time we've tried/sticking by something when it's failed twice:
'Why do you think this husband will stick around?' 'Well, third time's a charm...right? Right?'

Running out of time – you don't have as much time as you'd like:
'We're running out of time – please get dressed or we'll miss the bus!'

Spend your time wisely – make priorities in life:
'When you go to a festival, it's important to spend your time wisely. Go to the mojito line first, and then see the bands!'

It is just a matter of time – something is sure to happen at some time in the (near) future:
'It is just a matter of time before she realizes that her inflatable boyfriend won't be welcome at the Thanksgiving table this year.'

Killing time – spending/wasting time while you are waiting for something or someone:
'While I was waiting for my lunch date, I killed some time admiring footwear.'

Time is money – time is just as valuable as currency, so don't waste it:
'Please come in, you're late for my lesson. Time is money!'

Time is up – we've run out of time...and we have! This is the end of this list, folks!

03. 'TIME IS ON YOUR SIDE. YES IT IS.'

PROBLEM:
'My train left in time...on time...um...'

DIAGNOSIS:
We all get confused between *in time* and *on time*. This person should have said, 'My train left on time.' (If, in fact, it actually did leave on time.) There's a big difference between *on time* and *in time*.

On time means 'according to schedule' – not late and not early. 'The 9.35 train left on time' means that the train left at 9.35. 'The 9.35 train didn't leave on time' means that the train left later (or earlier!!) than scheduled. Your meetings, concerts, and movies should all start on time! Can someone please tell Rihanna? 'Rihanna made her fans wait three hours, so her show didn't start on time.' Shame on you, Rihanna! (This actually happened in Boston, on May 6, 2013.)

In time means 'enough time to do something'. 'I want to wake up in time to see the sun rise.' (For the record, I have NEVER said this.) 'She wants to get to the office in time to grab the best donut before anyone else does.' (For the record, I HAVE said this.) You can also say 'just in time' – 'She arrived at the opera just in time for the first aria.' However, if you say 'just on time', that sounds kind of weird. Just so you know.

REMEDY:
Think of what you are describing. Do you mean 'not late'? Then say *on time*. Do you mean 'enough time to do something'? Then use *in time*. You can be super-smart and use them both in a sentence: 'She didn't wake up in time to catch her train, because the train left on time!'

Wist je dat er ook een groot verschil is tussen '*in the end*' en '*at the end*'? '*In the end*' betekent 'eindelijk' of 'na een lange tijd':
'*In the end, after studying sushi rolling for four years, I finally got my ~~Masters~~ master's degree.*'

'*At the end*' is vrij letterlijk naar het Nederlands te vertalen als 'aan het eind' – het punt waarop iets is afgelopen:
'*I loved that musical, but the dance routines at the end were kind of lame.*'

Extra Vitamins!

We use *overtime* to talk about working longer than your usual or scheduled hours:
'*I've been working overtime to pay for my concert tickets.*'

We also have 'overtime pay', which is the money you get for working overtime. This is sometimes more than your usual wage:
'I hope I get lots of overtime pay for taking over her shift this week!'

It can also be a period of playing time added after the normal game time has finished:
'They had to go into overtime, and the winner won on penalty shots. It was such an exciting game!'

04. 'I LOVE IT! JUST DON'T BRING ME ANY...'

PROBLEM:
'Do you like some coffee?'

DIAGNOSIS:
Do you like is used instead of *would you like* when offering something to someone. In this case, someone was offering me coffee. Which I love. However, I didn't actually want any coffee at that particular moment. Because it was gin o'clock.

REMEDY:
Do you like means *Do you enjoy* something. This is used correctly when you are asking someone if they *like* something in general. 'Do you like coffee?' means 'Do you enjoy drinking coffee?' The answer to this could be yes or no. It's expressing a personal preference. You can also use it in different ways:

'Do you like sports?'
'Which do you like more, wine or beer?'
'Do you like the way he is looking at you? That's scary!'

The answers to questions like these are usually yes, no, or 'Oh my god, he's freaking me out!' However, *Would you like* is used when you are *offering* something to someone. If you ask, 'Would you like some coffee?' you are asking someone if they would like you to get them some coffee at that moment. You are offering them something, not asking about a general preference. I can't tell you how often someone has asked me 'Do you like coffee?' and then they show up with coffee. Very kind, very well intended, but still.

Extra Vitamins!

If you want someone to do something for you, there are different ways to ask. Let's make a list (and this time when I say 'let's' I actually mean 'me', but don't get used to that), going from most formal (like if you are talking to the king) to the most informal:

'Would you mind opening the window, please?'
'Would you open the window, please?'
'Could you open the window, please?'
'Can you open the window, please?'
'Would you please open the window?'
'Could you please open the window?'
'Can you please open the window?'
'Please open the window.'
'Open the window, please.'
'Open the window.'
'Goddammit, open the fucking window!'
'Piss off, I'll just do it myself.'

Are you surprised? Did you see some patterns here? That *would* is more formal than *could*, which is more formal than *can*? And that if you start a request with *please*, you are actually more direct than if you end the request with please? When I train people on this, they are often shocked, as the whole time they thought they were being polite, but they were actually being quite rude. Once a client looked at me, full of shame, and said 'For 20 years I have been saying, "Please can you…" for everything. Now I know why my British colleagues responded the way they did! I shame me dead!' I didn't have the heart to make him even more depressed by telling him he should have said 'I'm so ashamed!' (He'll know when he reads this book!)

05. 'NEVER LIE TO YOUR DOCTOR!'

PROBLEM:
'My sister is lying in the hospital.'

DIAGNOSIS:
This person uses *lying* to show that his sister is in the hospital. This, however, has another interpretation in English. The above sentence would most likely be interpreted to mean that she is in the hospital, and she's not telling the truth. This is wrong. You should always tell the truth, especially when dealing with medical professionals! Another reason why this is wrong is the use of the word *lying*. This common mistake comes from the Dutch use of *staan, zitten*, and *liggen* to show where things are. In English, we normally use *in*, *on* and *at* to show location.

REMEDY:
If someone is *in* the hospital, they are there as a patient:
'My brother has been in the hospital for a week now.'
'Her mother fell in love with a handsome surgeon while she was in the hospital for her sex-change operation.'

If someone is *at* the hospital, they are visiting someone or working there:
'I ran into an old colleague of mine at the hospital today.'
'I heard they are serving pea soup at the hospital today – let's sneak in and try some!'

You can remember the difference easily by remembering that *in* is short for *inside*, and *at* can be short for *at work*. Hope that helps! Oh, and by the way, my dear, your keys are not sitting in your purse, unless you have tiny little chairs in your purse for them to sit on. If you do, send me a picture. Thanks!

We talked a bit about *prepositions* (voorzetsels) in section 2, but here's some more information that might be helpful for you. When we talk about *future time*, we often use *in*. I often hear Dutch people say 'over a week'. Someone once said to me

'I'm going on vacation over a week.' The only appropriate response, of course, was 'Oh, how lovely! I'm going on vacation over a rainbow!'. She looked at me strangely. For a long time. But hey, I'm used to that. These sentences are correct:
'I'll see you in a week.'
'He is going on holiday in three days.'

If you want to talk about something happening before a certain moment in time, you can use the word 'within'. It's almost like another way of saying 'hopefully before':
'She hopes to lose five kilos within a month.'
'He'd like to stop his bingo addiction within a year.'
'You need to have that report finished within 24 hours.'

Notice how these are all used with a period of time (a month, a year, 24 hours)? If you want to have a date, or a specific time, use the preposition 'by' instead:
'She hopes to lose five kilos by Christmas.'
'He'd like to stop his bingo addiction by 2014.'
'You need to have that report finished by Friday afternoon.'

UNTIL OF TILL

Eindelijk eens een grammaticaal dilemma waar je je geen zorgen over hoeft te maken: *until* en *till* betekenen exact hetzelfde. Woohoo! Tegenwoordig wordt *till* vaak gebruikt als de verkorte vorm van *until*. Maar: let op de spelling! Hier gaat het vaak fout. *Until* wordt geschreven met één l, maar *till* heeft er opeens twee. Ze betekenen beide hetzelfde, namelijk *tot*:
'They decided to fight till the death to defend her honor.'
'The stores are open till 9 P.M. on Fridays.'
'The opera started at 8 and went on until 11 P.M.'

Wanneer *till* of *until* worden gebruikt in een negatieve zin kunnen ze ook *totdat* betekenen:
'He never knew how delicious a gin and tonic could be until he fell in love with a bartender.'
'She didn't realize that grammar was so sexy until she bought that book.'
'Until she met Harry, Sally always thought men were jerks.'

06. 'THANKS FOR SHARING.'

PROBLEM:
'Here's a picture of my boss. He's a pretty long guy.'

DIAGNOSIS:
This female employee was trying to tell me that her boss was tall. Instead, she told me he had a long penis. Now we know how she got the job!

REMEDY:
When we talk about how *long* someone is, we do not mean his or her height. If I had a dollar for every time I hear 'My brother is longer than me', 'Your husband is much longer than you said he was', or (yes, I heard this) 'One day I hope my son will be as long as his father', I would be living on my own private island off the coast of Tilburg. People. Let's not do this anymore. Think HEIGHT. Say that someone is TALL. (I am even making the letters TALLER for you to help you remember this!) Save talking about length for...other situations. OK? Promise you won't make this mistake anymore? Thank you!

Extra vitamins!

Let's work on expanding your vocabulary. Can you think of other ways to describe someone being tall? You can say someone is 'statuesque', 'lanky', 'towering', or just...'not short'. If you use the great site www.thesaurus.com, you will be able to increase your vocabulary fast. Many English words are overused, meaning they are used so often that they have lost their impact to some degree. To me, the words 'nice', 'good' and 'big' all have become quite bland. Let's see if we can come up with some other alternatives. Here's some to get you started:

NICE:
lovely, delightful, pleasant, pleasurable, warm, gentle, polite, kind, etc.
Can you hear a difference?
'The party was nice.'
'The party was delightful.'

The second sentence gives a clearer description about the party. It has more impact and creates a more vivid picture in your mind. At least it does to me.

Let's try another:

GOOD:
'His songs are good.'
'His songs are well crafted.'
See how the second sentence is more specific? That's what we're going for here.

BIG:
'Her shoes were big.'
'Her shoes were gargantuan.'
Whoa. Gargantuan? I love that word – it makes me think of Godzilla. Always a good thing.

And actually, to be honest, there is one moment in your life that the whole world knows how long you are, and people celebrate this fact with a sense of great joy and pride. I have even gotten beautifully designed cards announcing this wondrous fact: 'He's 53 centimeters long!'

This is on your birth announcement. When you are born, your doctor measures how long you are. After that, my darling, the chances of you ever being 53 centimeters long are over.

07. 'THIS IS A NIGHTMARE…'

PROBLEM:
'This night I didn't sleep very well.'

DIAGNOSIS:
I am confused. This person said *this night*, which makes me think he or she means 'tonight', which hasn't happened yet. However, 'I didn't sleep' is in the *past tense*

(verleden tijd), describing something that's finished. What's going on here?? This sounds like a grammatical nightmare. Maybe that's why she didn't sleep well?

REMEDY

If you're thinking of *vannacht* in Dutch, that's not 'this night'. As I mentioned before, we don't use 'this night' in this way. We could say something like 'This is a night to remember' or 'This is the best night ever!' But 'this night' as a time period? I think not. If something happened before you woke up, then say *last night*:
'Last night I dreamt of San Pedro.'
'She broke up with her boyfriend last night.'
'Did you see the moon last night? It was awesome!'

If you want to talk about something that's happening now (if it's the evening), or going to happen later this evening, then say *tonight*:
'Tonight's gonna be a good night.'
'I will call him tonight to discuss the new proposal.'
'I have never loved you more than I do tonight, and that has nothing to do with that huge mojito you just bought me.'

Extra vitamins!

We use *tonight* to talk about things that are going to happen this evening. We can use different verbs to talk about things happening in the future. I often get asked about the difference between *will* and *going to* – both used for future situations. You can say 'I *will* call him tonight' or 'I'm *going to* call him tonight.' Both are correct; it just depends on how certain you want to sound. If you use *will*, it usually means that it's a spontaneous, unplanned decision:
'Oh, I forgot to call him back! I will do that tonight.'
'Did you say you were thirsty? I'll get you something to drink!'

Will can also be used to show that a situation is unsure:
'Maybe I will visit Africa one day.'
'I hope I will get better at Rollerblading soon.'

Going to is used for things that are more planned and less uncertain. It's used a lot to describe intentions:
'I'm going to lose five kilos this year.'
'He's going to find a new job soon, as he's had lots of headhunters calling him.'

Let's see how these are used in a conversation:
Tiffany says to her dad, Fred: 'My bike has a flat tire – can you help me?' and her dad says, 'Sure, little muffin nose, I'll help you as soon as I finish my Sudoku.' A few minutes later, Tiffany's mom says, 'Fred, will you go to the store and buy me a can of Spam? I'm making something special for dinner!' Fred then says, 'I'm going to help Tiffany first, and then I'll help you. Sigh. Women.'

08. 'REMIND ME TO REMIND YOU TO REMEMBER...SOMETHING?'

PROBLEM:
'Can you remember me what the homework is?'

DIAGNOSIS:
No. I cannot. I cannot remember you anything. I am happy to remind you, but that's all I can do for you. Hope that works for you!

REMEDY:
People often get *remind* and *remember* confused. There's a big difference. *Remember* means to think about something from the past again. It's often used with *when*, *where*, *how*, and *why*. You don't need to say who or what brought back the memory, you just say that it happened:
'She suddenly remembered that she left the oven on when she came home to a kitchen full of smoke.'
'He remembered to grab his laptop case before leaving the house.'
'They didn't remember to put on sunscreen and now they look like lobsters!'

Remind is used in a completely different way. It's used to make someone think of something again. *Remind* on its own as a verb is wrong. You can say 'Please remember that,' but you can't say 'Please remind that'. You always need a person

(please remind me/him/her) and what you are asking them to do (take out the garbage/water the plants/buy Buffi a Ferrari):
'She reminded me that I had an important appointment with the Stamp Collecting Committee on Wednesday – I wouldn't want to forget that!'
'Please don't remind me why I thought getting a Smurf tattooed on my ankle was a good idea.'

You also can say that someone or something reminds you of someone else:
'You really remind me of my cousin – you both have curly red hair!'
'Your brother reminds me of a caveman – I've never seen anyone eat like that!'

09. 'I HAVE 99 PROBLEMS, AND *MUCH* AND *MANY* ARE TWO OF THEM.'

PROBLEM:
'I had much problems yesterday.'

DIAGNOSIS:
There are two grammar mistakes here, so maybe this person had more problems than she thought! She confused *much* and *many*, and used *much* in a positive statement, when *much* is normally used in a negative statement.
It's too easy for me to tell you the difference between *much* and *many*. I know that you'd want me to, but Buffi doesn't play that game. I will give you a list of words for each one and then you can tell me what the difference is. Let's go!

Much – time, energy, violence, rain, advice, money.
Many – people, children, flowers, tables, asses, donkeys.

If you look carefully, and think about it, you will see that the words for *much* are not used in the *plural form* (meervoud) (we don't say 'times', 'monies', etc.), and the words for *many* are used in the plural form. The words used with *much* are what we call *uncountable nouns* (ontelbare zelfstandig naamwoorden) and the words with *many* are *countable* (telbaar). This means you can walk into a room and count the number of donkeys, for example. (I don't know how often you have donkeys in your room, but it's always handy to know this anyway.)

REMEDY:
Think about what you are describing – is it countable or uncountable? Countable? Use *many*. Uncountable? Use *much*. And watch out: we usually use phrases with *much* in the negative form:
'I didn't have much time yesterday.'
'She didn't have much money when she was a student.'
'He didn't give us much advice, so we had to figure it out on our own.'

If you are in doubt about *much* or *many*, no need to worry ever again. Why? I have a fabulous trick! It works for everything, and it's really easy to remember. If you don't know if you should use *much* or *many*, just say *a lot of*. It works every time, for countable AND uncountable nouns. Guaranteed.
'There were a lot of children sitting at the table.'
'A lot of money gets left behind at casinos.'
'They had a lot of fish in their aquarium.'

Extra vitamins!

Now...what about the *opposite* of *much* and *many*? For this, we use either *a little* or *a few*. But which one where? *A little* is used for things that are uncountable: 'a little time', 'a little money', 'a little rain'. *A few* is used for things you can count: 'a few children', 'a few flowers', or 'a few tables', for example.

Wanneer je *a little* zegt in combinatie met een telbaar zelfstandig naamwoord (countable noun) zoals 'flower', 'table', of 'child' refereer je aan de grootte van het zelfstandig naamwoord. Wanneer je *a little* zegt in combinatie met een ontelbaar zelfstandig naamwoord (uncountable noun) zoals 'money', 'time', of 'energy' refereer je aan de hoeveelheid van het zelfstandig naamwoord. Kijk maar eens naar de onderstaande zin:
She watched her children playing at the little table, and realized how little energy she had to play with them. That double mojito at lunch was not a good idea.

And guess what, darling? If you are in doubt about whether to use *a little* or *a few*, you know what to do, right? My fabulous trick also works here! If you are not sure which one to use, then just say *not a lot of* and you are good to go!

'There were not a lot of people attending the opening night of the six-hour Swiss German opera.'
'I don't have a lot of real friends, but I have tons of imaginary ones!'
'They didn't give him a lot of advice – they just told him to drop the gun.'

Easy, right?

Much en *many* worden gebruikt om te praten over het aantal of de hoeveelheid van dingen. We hebben het meervoud van het zelfstandig naamwoord nodig voor deze vorm ('children', 'people', 'beers', etc.). Maar wist je dat er enkele woorden in het Engels zijn *that get a little wacky* wanneer het aankomt op hun meervoudsvorm? Kijk hier eens naar:
one fish – two fish
one sheep – two sheep
one species – two species
one aircraft – two aircraft

We hebben zelfs een paar woorden die eindigen op een s in enkelvoud! Kijk maar:
jeans – My jeans are too tight – I can barely sit down!
glasses – Her glasses were thick and sexy.
trousers – His trousers were too loose because he went on a new algae diet and lost 41 kilos.

10. 'MAKE A TO-DO LIST...'

PROBLEM:
'I'm sorry, Buffi. I didn't make my homework last night.'

DIAGNOSIS:

Of course you didn't make your homework! I made your homework, silly! You meant to say that you 'didn't do' your homework. Which is pretty ironic, considering the homework was an exercise I created on the difference between *make* and *do*.

What's the difference? Oh, darling, you know me by now. It's much too easy for me to simply tell you. Let's get those brain cells burning for a second (OK, maybe five seconds) and really think about it. I will give you a list of things you *make*, and a list of things you *do*. Let's see if you can figure out the difference!

You *make*: a cake, a baby, lesson plans, arrangements, a design
You *do*: your homework, your duty, household chores (the laundry, the dishes, the vacuuming, etc.)

Can you spot the difference? If you *make* something, there is some bit of creativity or production involved; you are creating something. You put different things together and make something new:
'*My friends are coming over later, so I'm going to make a chocolate cake.*'
'*I saw her at the travel agency. She's making plans for her vacation.*'
'*I'm making a new design for my kitchen. I hope my kids like orange!*'

If you *do* something, you follow orders or instructions, or complete a task:
'*I'm too tired to do the laundry.*'
'*We have to do the dishes before my mother arrives!*'
'*You have to do your duty as a good citizen and report that crime! That unicorn thief needs to be stopped before he strikes again!*'

REMEDY:

Think of what you are trying to say — is there creation, construction, or production involved? Then use *make*. If you are just doing what someone told you to do (like I tell all my lovely students what they should do), or completing a task, then use *do*.

Extra Vitamins!

Here's a handy list of phrases with *make* or *do* to help you out a bit more:

Do:

do badly	*do time* (to go to prison)
do business	*do well*
do someone a favor	*do your best*
do good	*do your hair*
do harm	*do your nails*

Make:

make amends (to make up for doing something bad or wrong)	*make a mistake*
	make money
make arrangements	*make a move*
make believe (to pretend)	*make a noise*
make a decision	*make a payment*
make a difference	*make a phone call*
make an effort	*make a plan*
make an excuse	*make a point*
make a fool of yourself	*make a profit*
make a fortune	*make a promise*
make friends	*make a remark*
make a fuss	*make a sound*
make a journey	*make a speech*
make love	*make a suggestion*

So...*make* my day and *do* your best when it comes to learning English!

11. 'I'M GETTING USED TO THE FACT THAT I CAN NEVER GET USED TO THAT.'

PROBLEM:

'I'm used to smoking a lot, but I quit.'

DIAGNOSIS:

This person got confused between *used to smoke* and *used to smoking*. There's a big difference between them! If you *used to do* something, this means that you don't do it anymore. For example:

'I used to make lots of mistakes in English, but that stopped the moment this book touched my grateful hands!'
'She used to bite her toenails but stopped when her husband said it was gross.'
'They used to play in that forest when they were kids – until they discovered that corpse.'

It can also be used (in the negative form) for something that once was true but no longer is:

'When I was a child, I didn't used to like gin, but now I really do!' (Hypothetically speaking, of course!)
'It's so weird that she likes coffee now. She didn't used to like it.'

If you say *used to doing* something, this means nearly the opposite. It means a general habit or something that happens on a regular basis:

'I'm used to speaking excellent English because Buffi saved my ass.'
'He got used to her snoring after three years.'
'I'll never get used to the sound of Miley Cyrus rapping.'

REMEDY:

Use *used to do* for things that you don't do anymore, and *used to doing* for things that are still normal to you. Or get freaky and use them both in one sentence!
'I'm used to drinking gin now, but I used to drink wine!' (So she said.)

Extra Vitamins!

Getting used to means adjusting to the idea of something, or adapting to a new situation.
'I'm just getting used to the idea that my new blue mohawk isn't as great as I thought it was!'
'He's trying to get used to the idea that his new girlfriend was actually born a boy.'
'They just have to get used to the idea that tonic tastes better with gin.'

In de Engelse taal hebben we het gezegde *'It takes some getting used to.'* Dit wordt gebruikt wanneer iets in eerste instantie niet zo leuk is, maar na een tijdje niet zo erg meer is:

'Eating hot Thai peppers might take some getting used to, but after a while you get used to the taste. Now please pass me some water!'

'Naked horseback riding does take some getting used to, but you don't notice the pain after a while.'

12. 'MIGHT BE MORE INTERESTING IF YOU TURNED IT ON FIRST.'

PROBLEM:
'Last night I looked TV.'

DIAGNOSIS:
There are two problems here. (Actually, three. Two are English-related, and one is that this person had really bad breath while he was saying this. But I'll focus on the English part.) The first grammatical mistake is using *looked* instead of *watched*. The second is that *look* needs to be followed by *at* when it means examining:

'I looked at his face and realized he was not as handsome as I thought.' If you use *look* to mean appearance – 'You look lovely today!' – then no *at* is necessary.

There's a big difference between *to look at* and *to watch*. If you 'look at' something, you are examining its appearance. You usually look at things that are not moving. For example, you can look at a picture, a photograph, or a painting. Someone can ask you *to have a look at* something — this means that they want you to examine something. 'Can you *have a look at* this contract, please?'

If you watch something, however, you are focused on the action involved. You watch a movie, sports, or children playing. This person should have said, 'Last night I *watched* TV,' or 'I *watched* TV last night.'

REMEDY:
Think about what you are talking about. If there is action, motion, or movement involved, use *watch*. If not, use *look at*. If you look at the TV, it's usually a lot more fun if you turn it on first!

If someone says 'Look at her!', they want you to check out her appearance: 'Look at her! She's wearing that new Justin Bieber bra!' If someone says 'Watch her!', it usually sounds like some kind of warning: 'Watch her, because I think she's trying to drown your hamster!'.

On a side note, I get asked all the time if there's a difference between *Look out!* and *Watch out!* I can honestly say, after thinking about this for a long time, that there really isn't. Use whichever one works for you!

And what's a *lookout*? A *lookout* is someone who keeps watch while you're doing something that you shouldn't be doing. Like using bad grammar, for example! The *lookout* might say 'Look out! The grammar police are coming to get you!' However, since you're reading this awesome book, your ass is saved, so you don't need to worry!

Extra Vitamins!

We have several expressions that use *to look* that can be either literal (letterlijk) or figurative (figuurlijk). In a figurative sense, to *look down on* means to think that someone is not as good as you are, or to feel superior to someone:
'She has looked down on my family my whole life because she's the richest girl in town.'

Here it's used literally:
'She looked down while walking across the high bridge in stilettos and got very nervous.'

To look up in a figurative sense:
'I have always looked up to people who follow their dreams.'

And in a literal sense:
'She looked up from her newspaper to find a handsome stranger staring at her.'

To see betekent dat er een afbeelding op je netvlies tevoorschijn komt: het gaat over een fysieke mogelijkheid.
'She didn't see well enough so she decided to get glasses. Now she's a sexy nerd.'
'Did you see Phil's new hipster beard? It rocks!'

To see kan echter ook begrijpen betekenen:
'Oh, so 14 brownies mysteriously disappeared late last night? I see.'
'Can you see what the problem is? That vinegar-flavored ice cream really bombed!'

13. 'NICE ASS!'

PROBLEM:
'If you look closely, you'll see that this chair has a beautiful backside.'

DIAGNOSIS:
A well-known designer was showing me a photo of a chair from his new spring collection in one of our lessons. The chair, indeed, was beautiful. However, I could not determine how lovely the backside was until the designer himself turned around. Someone's *backside* is his or her ass. I actually asked him to turn around in the lesson, to demonstrate what his mistake was, and the look on his face was priceless. A chair has only a *front* or a *back*. That's it. This is also true for books, envelopes, cars, airplanes, buses, rooms, and so many other things. None of these will ever have a backside.

REMEDY:
You put your *backside* against the *back* of a chair when you sit down. Maybe that will help you remember it easily.

Since this book is all about saving your...backside, how about we have some fun and make a list of all the different ways you can say *backside*?

arse *(UK English)*
ass *(obviously)*
behind
bum
buns
buttocks
can
cheeks
derriere *(This one sounds so fancy!)*

fanny *(Watch out! This is slang for vagina in UK English!)*
keister *(pronounced 'keester', used more in US than UK)*
rear end
tush
tushie
tuchus *(Yiddish)*

And, darling, I couldn't leave this without expanding your educational horizon with some lovely expressions that involve the word ass. I actually suspect that this might be the real reason that some of you bought this book!

Ass clown: a fool
'Stop being such an ass clown and help me put this bookcase together!'
Ass backwards: wrong or in the wrong order
'Great! Now you've done this ass backwards and the shelves are vertical!'
Ass is grass: the state of being in trouble
'Shit, man, I can't believe I stole that police car last night. My ass is grass.'
Ass man: Someone who prefers bottoms to breasts when admiring women
'Kim K. only dated ass men, obviously.'
Ass on the line: being responsible for something
'You better not screw this one up – it's my ass on the line if you do!'
Asshole: an extremely unpleasant person
'Stop being such an asshole and give me that Tinkerbell cupcake RIGHT NOW.'
Badass: someone you don't want to mess with
'He thinks he's such a badass because he rides a Harley.'
Bet your ass: assert that something is definitely true
'I'll be at your strip poker game on Friday. You can bet your ass on it!'
Get your ass in gear: get moving
'Get your ass in gear, otherwise we will miss our flight!'
Give a rat's ass: to not care (always used in the negative)
'I don't give a rat's ass about who broke that vase, you have to clean it up before Obama sees it!'

Have your head up your ass: to be clueless
'He really had his head up his ass thinking that his cheek implants would look natural.'
Kiss my ass!: Screw you!
'If you don't like my Barbie Fairy cake, then you can just kiss my ass!'

Well, my dear, looks like you've completed chapter 1! Well done! I hope you laughed your ass off and learned something new.

DON'T GO THERE

I beg of you. What you are about to read are all common mistakes that I've heard way too often, often made by my students or my clients. They are really funny, so let's laugh about them, but let's also learn why they don't work in English. I mean, they DO work...if you want to sound perverted or lame.
And yes, I have heard (or read) every single one of these!

THINGS MY STUDENTS SAY (BUT ONLY ONCE!)
'*Mag ik vrijstelling voor Engels, Buffi?*'
'What is "*vrijstelling*" in English?'
'Freestyling?'
'No. And no.'

Vrijstelling means exemption from a lesson or class. I did make him freestyle for me, though. He turned out to be an excellent rapper!

From a student's marketing plan:
'The best way to promote your band is by mouth to mouth.'
I love this one. Yes, if you are able to save lives by mouth-to-mouth resuscitation, otherwise known as CPR, then please talk about how good your band is while you are blowing into someone's mouth to give them the breath of life. By all means! However, if you just want people to talk about how great your band is, just use word of mouth. That's probably much more effective!

'Thank you for being such a good teacher. You really learned me a lot.'
Actually, my dear, I didn't learn you anything. I taught you a thing or two (but obviously not enough). Still, I hope you learned from me. And yes, I also learned from you. Thank you for that!

'I have to do an intern for 140 hours and was hoping you could help me.'
Just a second, I'll get Bill Clinton on the line. If you are interested in doing an internship, however, then we can talk.

And on a related note...
'I have to walk the stage for three months.'
Either that's a really slow fashion show or you are trying to say you have an internship.

'My band meets in the repetition room every week.'
You meet in the rehearsal room. I repeat: you meet in the rehearsal room.

From a student from Spain:
'Every summer I spend most of my time lying on the bitch. Sometimes my wife comes with me and we lie on the bitch together.'
After laughing really hard, I gently told this lovely man that he needed to smile more when he said the word beach.

'I am here for the English screaming test today.'
Actually, I think I have made a student or two scream...during my screening test.

'I will be putting all the assignments in you on Friday.'
This scares me. I'm not even touching this one.

'I'm so sorry for messing your lesson yesterday.'
That's OK. My lessons are not always clean to begin with. I hope that you do show up next time, however. We wouldn't want to miss you!

CHAPTER 2

HAND AND MOUTH IMPROVEMENT

The first part of this chapter, 'Pronunciation Predicaments', deals with your gorgeous mouth and how to use it. Since this book is about ass saving, I have decided not to get into every pronunciation problem that could possibly exist in English. There are several other books and websites out there devoted specifically to that noble cause. I have decided, however, to share the **Dutch Top 3** – the three biggest mistakes people's mouths make when trying to speak English. Of course you're not doing anything wrong, it's your silly mouth that keeps messing it up! I hope you realize that your mouth is not alone in making these mistakes; there are thousands of others who have mouths like yours. Let's hope the owners of those mouths are all reading this book too.

Part 2 is 'Writing Washouts'. In this section I cover the basic mistakes people's hands make when writing letters and emails, and take it from there. The mistakes (of your hands, because you, my love, are completely innocent) and the corrections also apply to spoken English, of course, so please tell your mouth after finishing this part. I read these mistakes every single day, and they are so easy to correct. I hope that from now on you will be known as The Person Whose Hands Used To Write Incorrectly. That is my dream for you, my darling.

After your mouth and your hands have been saved, then it's time for 'Spell Check Yourself Before You Wreck Yourself.' English is easy...when you speak. However, when you write, it's a whole different story. One spelling mistake can cause laughter, shame, or embarrassment for hours to come (or even for the rest of your life, if it's inked on your body.) That's why I wanted to devote some of our valuable time to the most commonly made spelling mistakes. If you get to know these, you will never make people laugh hysterically while spitting up coffee all over their keyboard as they read your mail, or burst out in uncontrollable giggles as you swagger by with your brand new **'I AM AWSOME!'** tattoo.

Pronunciation Predicaments

14. 'ICE ICE BABY...'

PROBLEM:
'I see the lice in your ice.'

DIAGNOSIS:
Oy. Here this lovely person was singing a ballad about someone they loved who broke their heart. However, when I heard it, it made me feel even more sorry for him. What went wrong? In his ballad, the words *eyes* and *lies* are spoken with the *s* sound, instead of the correct way – with a slight *z* sound. If you mean 'I see the lies in your eyes' but say 'I see the lice in your ice', people will look at you like you've just poured a bottle of ketchup over your head. Or think that you've actually got tiny little bugs in your ice cubes. However, if you are in a situation where you do find bugs in your ice cubes, I highly recommend saying this sentence, and then calling the Health Department immediately.

The words *eyes, lies, criticize, analyze, surprise* and *hypnotize* (and many others) all end in a *z* sound. It's not a sharp sounding z, just a soft z. You don't need to over-emphasize this sound; it's just how we 'close' the word.

REMEDY:
Let's do this one in Dutch! Het verschil tussen de *s* en *z* klank ligt in het verschil in gebruik van je stembanden. Het gebruik van de *s* is precies hetzelfde als in het Nederlands. Echter, wanneer je de z klank wilt maken, gebruik je je stembanden, en bij de *s* klank worden ze niet gebruikt. Maar hoe weet je nu of je je stembanden gebruikt? Je kunt het voelen! Plaats je handen onder je kaak, aan beide kanten van je nek. Probeer het woord *buzz* te zeggen. Adem uit terwijl je het zegt, en houdt de z klank zo lang vast als je kunt – als je het goed doet, voel je een lichte trilling (een buzz) in dit gebied. Vervolgens houd je je handen waar ze zijn, en zeg je het woord *bus*. Adem uit, en houdt de *s* klank wederom zo lang vast als je kan. Wanneer je dit goed doet, voel je geen trilling onder je kaak. *Got it, darling?*

Zeg de volgende woorden hardop zo snel mogelijk achter elkaar en kijk of het je lukt je stembanden te sturen! Het eerste woord bevat een s-klank en het tweede woord een z-klank. Maar dat had je al wel door, toch? *Of course!*

advice/advise	*price/prize*
bus/buzz	*race/raise*
ice/eyes	*rice/rise*
lice/lies	*sip/zip*
loose/lose	*Sue/zoo*

Nu je deze woorden een beetje beheerst gaan we door naar niveau twee: de zinnen. Lukt het je om deze zinnen uit te spreken met een stille *s* en een trillende *z*? *You betcha!*

The rise in zoo prices was based on the advice of the consultant.
The prize for losing the most zippers went to Sue this year.
She sipped her rice wine and realized that it was too sour.
Sally saw seven seals swimming in the sea.
Seventeen sailors were seasick during the race to the bus station.

Extra Vitamins!

While we're at it, let's tackle another tricky pronunciation problem! I hear these words pronounced wrong all the time:

psychologist: sy-KO-lo-gist
psychology: sy-KO-lo-gee
psychiatrist: sy-KIY-a-trist
psychiatry: sy-KIY-a-tree
psychiatric: sy-ki-A-trik

What do these all have in common? They all start with the *sy* sound. The *p* sound is silent. Yes, always.

Let's try (oh, and whenever I say 'let's', I mean you) to say these fun sentences:
'The psychologist tried to get psyched up for her exam, but she was scared because her psychiatrist gave her the wrong medication the day before.'
'Psychiatric nurses have to work very hard to improve the psychological mindset of their patients.'

Wist je dat er in het Engelse woord *architect* helemaal geen *ch* klank zit? Je spreekt het uit als 'ar-key-tekt'. Gelukkig is deze heel makkelijk te onthouden: denk gewoon aan het moment waarop jij de key kreeg voor het prachtige nieuwe huis dat hij voor je ontwierp!

Laten we verdergaan met een andere groep woorden waar veel mensen problemen mee hebben: woorden met een stille *b*.

debt – wordt uitgesproken als *det*
doubt – wordt uitgesproken als *dout*
lamb – wordt uitgesproken als *lam*
limb – wordt uitgesproken als *lim*
numb – wordt uitgesproken als *num*

plumber – wordt uitgesproken als *plummer*
subtle – wordt uitgesproken als *suttel*
thumb – wordt uitgesproken als *thum*
tomb – wordt uitgesproken als *tuum*
womb – wordt uitgesproken als *wuum*

Dan nu weer door naar het tweede level: lukt het je om onderstaande zinnen op te zeggen?
'The lamb emerged from the womb and caused the vet to doubt that the zebra was actually the father.'
'The plumber moved subtly through the kitchen so as not to disturb the Egyptian mummy who was resting in his tomb.'
'I doubt you will ever lose a limb or a thumb while climbing, but I certainly hope that you are numb if it ever happens.'
'He was so much in debt that he had to sell all his crumbs, which made him feel so dumb.'

15. 'I THINK I SAW THAT IN *THE WIZARD OF OZ*?'

PROBLEM:
'I'm going on vacation with tree friends.'

DIAGNOSIS:
This lovely person did not say the *th* sound in three correctly, which makes me think that they hang out in the forest way too much!

REMEDY:
Aangezien dit onderwerp al moeilijk genoeg is, ga ik nu maar even over op het Nederlands. De TH-klank is een van de meest moeilijke klanken om te maken in het Engels. En, om het je allemaal nog makkelijker te maken: we hebben eigenlijk *twee* vormen van de TH-klank: zonder stem en met stem. Over dit verschil leren de meeste mensen niets op school, dus mensen zijn vaak verrast wanneer ik ze dit vertel. Je kunt het verschil tussen de TH-klanken als volgt voelen in je eigen lichaam: plaats je handen onder je kaaklijn, zodat je je stembanden voelt. Laten we ons eerst focussen op woorden met een TH-klank *zonder stem*. Dit betekent dat wanneer je de woorden correct uitspreekt, je *geen trilling* voelt onder je kaaklijn. Steek je tong uit tot voorbij je tanden wanneer je de TH-klank maakt, en probeer de klank zo lang mogelijk vast te houden terwijl je uitademt. Probeer het met deze woorden: *with, both, path, math, three*. Als je geen trilling voelde, heb je het goed gedaan! Yeah for you! Laten we nu eens de TH-klank *met stem* proberen. Plaats je handen terug onder je kaaklijn en steek je tong opnieuw uit tot voorbij je tanden. Probeer de volgende woorden te zeggen: *mother, brother, other, these, those*. Voelde je *trilling* onder je kaaklijn en een licht gekietel op je lippen? Dan heb je het goed gedaan! You rock!

Here is a list of words with the *th* blown or buzzed (zonder stem en met stem, dus) at the beginning, in the middle, and at the end. This is a good way to determine if you have problems in a particular area. Some words have a blown *th* sound, and others have a buzzed *th* sound. Can you figure out which is which?

Beginning:	Middle:	End:
this	other	with
that	mother	path
these	brother	bath
those	either	moth
think	rather	both
thing	gather	cloth
three	smother	broth
thank	something	death
Thursday	anything	sloth*
throw	although	math

*A sloth is a three-toed animal which is very, very slow. We often refer to someone as a 'sloth' if they are behaving like a lazy pig.

Try saying these words back to back:

moth/moss	thick/sick
mouth/mouse	thing/sing
path/ass	think/sink
tenth/tense	thumb/sum
theme/seem	worth/worse

Extra vitamins!

Tongue twisters are a great way to force yourself to concentrate on the difference between the two forms of the *th* sound in English. No matter how old you are, tongue twisters are always lots of fun! Try saying these sentences a million times, as fast as you can. Then force someone you love to do the same and hug them at the end when they screw it up.

- 'Those three fathers think that anything is threatening their treat.'
- 'Thank you for thinking that Thursday was my birthday! I certainly thought I was thirty!'
- 'Three thousand three hundred and thirty three thirsty dirty thieves threw the cloth through the threatening trees.'
- 'Thank you for that fifth cup of broth!'
- 'They were tired but thought that anything was better than nothing.'
- 'The things that he brought showed that the moth was not the father.'
- 'Anything you throw will be three times thanked.'

16. 'FROM BUFFI WIT LOF!'

PROBLEM:
'I lof you.' (This is actually very lovely; it's not *really* a problem. The person who said this to me is very kind, extremely attractive, famously talented, and fabulous...but still. His pronunciation...oy vey!)

DIAGNOSIS:
This gorgeous creature meant to say 'I love you.' Or perhaps he actually meant to say 'I lof you' because he thinks I look sexy with grey hair from worrying about his English so much.

REMEDY:
De *v* klank klinkt in het Engels veel harder dan in het Nederlands. Het is gelukkig niet moeilijk te leren! Plaats je ringvinger in het midden van je onderlip. Zeg het woord *love* en adem uit terwijl je de *v* klank uitspreekt. Als je dit goed doet, zou je je onderlip moeten voelen trillen. Oké, zeg nu het woord *very*, en houd de *v* klank zo lang als je kan vast. Ben je nog steeds aan het trillen? *Excellent!* Houd je vinger daar en zeg nu het woord *fast* – houd de *f* klank zo lang vast als je kan. Nu zou je *geen trilling* (op je onderlip) moeten voelen terwijl je het zegt. Probeer het eens met een van mijn favoriete woorden, *fabulous!* Geen trilling? *Well done!*

SECTION ONE

Extra vitamins!

Now let's try them back to back and see if you can feel the difference:

believe/belief	veil/fail
leave/leaf	very/ferry
prove/proof	vast/fast*
vague/fake	vein/feign**

---

* **vast/fast**

Weet je wat *vast* betekent? Het betekent *weids*:
'Texas is known for having vast fields.'
... Oooh! Did you see what I did there? I just used *v* and *f* back to back in that sentence! Now you try!

** **vein/feign**

Weet je wat *feign* betekent? Het betekent *veinzen*, doen alsof.
'He feigned a migraine to get out of his test.'

Now grab a sexy friend and look deeply into his or her eyes and say these sentences. Who said pronunciation exercises couldn't be romantic?
- 'They didn't believe that the proof was very relevant. They thought it was very fake.'
- 'Four very fast vans drove through the ferry parking lot and frightened various friends.'
- 'Half of the vines were not safe for a few viewers.'
- 'The volcano in Virginia forced the farmers to vary their crops for the following summer.'
- 'He played his violin with such violence that his friends were forced to finish his part.'
- 'She vacuumed the floral carpet with such verve that she forced her femur into a frenzy.'

Er zijn sommige woorden die de *f* klank hebben, terwijl er helemaal geen *f* in het woord zit. *Crazy but true!* Probeer deze woorden eens uit te spreken:

cough	laugh
enough	rough
graph	tough

Writing Washouts

17. 'DON'T TALK LIKE YODA*.'

* Don't know who Yoda is? Time to check out the original Star Wars...preferably on a VHS system to get the full effect.

PROBLEM:
'Tomorrow to the movies we go.'

DIAGNOSIS:
The word order here (and the verb form) is wrong. The correct way to say this sentence is 'We are going to the movies tomorrow.' However, if you want to sound like Yoda, keep talking like this. I'm sure some chicks will dig it.

REMEDY:
English word order has a basic pattern. We have a very simple way of making English sentences, and towards the end of this section we will get more complicated for our die-hard sexy grammar nerds! Here we go:

The most basic word order pattern is this one:
SUBJECT–VERB–PLACE–TIME
(onderwerp)–(werkwoord)–(plaats)–(tijd)

'She is meeting him in Amsterdam next Thursday.'

We start with the *subject* (onderwerp): who or what is the sentence about? – 'she'. Generally speaking, the subject is the most important part of the sentence, so we start with that first. I always think that Dutch people are so patient because it seems to me that the subject of the sentence is often towards the end of a sentence. For example: *Vandaag, in ons wekelijks overleg, gaat Stijn ons vertellen over het nieuwe computersysteem.* You see?! They have to keep on waiting to find out what it's actually about. Kudos for being so patient, Dutchies!

SECTION ONE   55

After the subject, we have the *verb* (werkwoord): the action in the sentence, *is meeting*, then the *place* (plaats) *Amsterdam*, and then we end with the *time* (tijd), *next Thursday*.

Here are some more examples:
'He's flying to Paris on Friday.'
'They kissed in the supermarket last week.'
'I go skiing in Las Vegas every winter – water skiing.'

If you start an English sentence with the time, it usually means that the time is the most essential part of the sentence, even more than the subject. This could be important – for example, if the police are questioning you. You could then say something like 'At 4.15 I opened my door, and at 4.17 I heard a gunshot, and at 4.20 I found my poor goldfish lying dead on the floor.' However, in normal conversations, feel free to put the time situation at the end of the sentence.

In English word order, *place* usually comes before time. For example:
'They went to a birthday party last Saturday night.'
'I visited New York in May.'
'They've lived in the same house for over 20 years.'

Now let's take it to the next level. There are other parts of an English sentence that have a particular order. For example, you might have an *object* (lijdend voorwerp). An object receives the action of the verb, and comes after the verb in a sentence. This is what it looks like when we add an object to a sentence:

SUBJECT–VERB–OBJECT–PLACE–TIME
(onderwerp)–(werkwoord)–(lijdend voorwerp)–(plaats)–(tijd)

'She wrote a letter last week.'
'He reads a newspaper every morning.'
'I bought some awesome shoes yesterday!'

Now let's move on to something really sexy called *adverbs of frequency (bijwoord van frequentie)*. These are words that talk about how *often* you do something. Some of the most frequently used ones are *always, sometimes, never, usually, often,* and *seldom*. These words come before the verb in an English sentence.

SUBJECT–ADVERB OF FREQUENCY–VERB–OBJECT–PLACE–TIME
(onderwerp)–(bijwoord van 'frequentie')–(werkwoord)–(lijdend voorwerp)–(plaats)–(tijd)

'I always go to work by bus.'
'He never smokes in the car.'
'We often go disco bowling on Saturdays.'

If your verb is made up of two words, these words go in the middle:
'I have never been to Scotland.'
'We will always remember how much you helped us.'
'He could never visit the zoo when he was a child.'

OK. Now we know that if you use *always, sometimes, never,* or other adverbs of frequency, they all go before the main verb. (If your verb is made up of two verbs, the main verb is the second verb – has *been*, had *studied*, will *go*, etc.) However, if your verb stems from *to be* (which is a pretty freaky verb, as it doesn't follow the normal grammar rules – ooh, *to be*, you rebel, you!), meaning that your verb is now *am, is, are, was,* or *were*, then the adverbs of frequency go after these verbs, not before.

We don't say 'He always is late to work', but:
'He is always late to work.'
'We are often at home.'
'I am never ill.'

Try to say the sentences above fast. What happens? If you do it correctly, then you will probably say 'He's...', 'We're...' and 'I'm...'. Well done! The only time we would reverse the order and say 'I never am' for example, is if you are answering a question:
'You're not often at home, are you?'
'No, I never am.'

SUBJECT–VERB–OBJECT–ADVERB OF MANNER–PLACE–TIME

(onderwerp)–(werkwoord)–(lijdend voorwerp)–(bijwoord van 'manier'*)–(plaats)–(tijd)

* *'Bijwoord van manier' bestaat natuurlijk niet, net als 'bijwoord van frequentie', maar ik noem ze toch even zo om het duidelijkheidsgehalte van mijn boek ietwat te verhogen. In het Nederlands worden de* adverb of manner *en de* adverb of frequency *beide geschaard onder de bijwoorden.*

If you have an adverb – a word which describes the manner of the action (how the action is done, usually ending in *ly*) in a sentence, it comes *before* the place and the time:
'He sang the aria beautifully at La Scala last night.'
'She drove quickly through the streets of LA on Sunday morning.'
'I played tennis badly at my tournament last weekend.'

Can we put all of the elements together to make one amazing, fabulous, awesome (and correct!) English sentence? The chances of you needing every single element are quite low, but you never know...drum roll, please...

SUBJECT–ADVERB OF FREQUENCY–VERB–OBJECT–ADVERB OF MANNER–PLACE–TIME

(onderwerp)–(bijwoord van 'frequentie')–(werkwoord)–(lijdend voorwerp)–(bijwoord van 'manier')–(plaats)–(tijd)

'He often bakes cupcakes splendidly in his kitchen on weekends.'
'I always write my lesson plans carefully in my office every Sunday night.'

Extra vitamins!

Word order can be flexible when it comes to talking about the date or the time. If you are making an appointment with someone, you can start with the day of the week, then the date, and then the time. For example, 'Our appointment is on Monday, April 3rd, at 10.30.' Another option is to start with the time and then the date: 'I'll see you at 10.30 on Monday, April 3rd.'

In het Brits Engels komt het cijfer van de datum eerst en daarna pas de maand, net als in Nederland. In het Amerikaans Engels is het andersom: hier komt de maand eerst, en daarna pas het nummer!
Brits: *4 March* (oftewel 4/3)
Amerikaans: *March 4* (oftewel 3/4)
In hoofdstuk 11 vind je meer informatie over Brits vs Amerikaans Engels.

Choose whichever form works for you – just stay consistent!

18. 'IT TAKES...TWO...TOO...TO TANGO.'

PROBLEM:
'I love grammar to!'

DIAGNOSIS:
I actually read this. The good news was that I was thrilled to know that there was another Sexy Grammar Nerd out there, and that I was not alone in my quest to spread the Gospel of Great Grammar from the mountaintops (which can be quite a challenge to find in the Netherlands). However, the bad news is that this person used the wrong word. I guess she didn't love grammar as much as she thought. Instead of writing *too*, she wrote *to*, which makes her comment even more ironic.

REMEDY:
These three words – *to, too,* and *two* – are called homonyms. That's sexy talk for words that sound exactly the same but have different meanings. Let's break it down. We have *two*, which means number 2:
'*His wife became suspicious when she came home to find two empty champagne glasses on the kitchen table.*'
'*I have two favorite foods; gin and tonic.*'

The word *too* can mean different things. It can mean 'also':
'*OMG! I love Ferraris too! Let's get one together!*'
'*She felt bad when she told him that she loved riding bareback too, because she had never done it before and was only trying to impress him with her equestrian skills.*'

Too can also mean excessive:
'He ate too much and felt ill after the party.'
'Those shoes are too expensive. I would wait until they are on sale.'

We also have *to*, which can be used to give direction:
'He went to the party after work, and then he went to bed.'
'I'd love to go to the movies with you, David Beckham. Thank you for asking.'

To can also be used as an *indirect object* (meewerkend voorwerp). That's sexy talk for answering the question 'To whom?':
'Please give that Hello Kitty pen to John when you're done.'
'Could you please stop talking to them?'

To can also mean 'until':
'The stores in town are open from Monday to Saturday.'
'The movie is from 8.30 to 10 tonight.'

Did you know that in America, if a child says 'I have to go number two', this means that they have to poop? You didn't? Now you do. ('To go number one' means to pee, by the way.)

I live to educate.

Extra vitamins!

We have lots of other homonyms in English, just to make life even more interesting for you. A common group is *there, they're,* and *their*. People get these confused all the time, too. Let's sort this one out right away:

There means not here:
'Please move those boxes over there — they are in the way.'
'Can you see that building over there? I used to live there.'

They're is short for they are:
'They're coming over for dinner in 10 minutes! Quick! Grab something out of the freezer and throw it in the microwave!'
'They're always coming up with new technology – I can't seem to keep up!'

Their means belonging to them:
'My parents sold their boat last week.'
'Their story really made me laugh – I mean, who knew that he was really a circus clown in disguise?'

Another pair that drives people crazy is *affect* and *effect*. *Affect* is a *verb* (werkwoord) that means to produce a consequence or to influence:
'The whole town was affected by the floods.'
'Her new cologne, Eau de la Grammaire, affected the people in the elevator significantly.'

Effect is a *noun* (zelfstandig naamwoord). It is the consequence or the result of something:
'The effect of drinking decaf coffee was quite surprising to him.'
'I tried going to the gym more often, but it had no effect, as I was still eating ice cream for breakfast every day.'

19. 'LOOK OUT!'

PROBLEM:
'I look forward to *meet* you!'

DIAGNOSIS:
This person, although they meant well, probably forgot to write 'I look forward to *meeting* you!' I'm sure that's what happened. Yeah, that's what happened. They knew and then they forgot. Uh-huh.

REMEDY:
This is a very common problem in (written) English. I get countless emails every month ending with this lovely phrase. After *look forward to*, you need to use the

verb in the *ing* form afterwards. I could get really sexy and say that this *ing* form is called a gerund, and has something to do with a prepositional object, but I won't go there. Just know that after the phrase *look forward to*, you always need the *ing* form of the verb:
'I look forward to meeting you next week.'
'I look forward to receiving your products.'
'I look forward to finally getting my cat-grooming diploma later this year!'

You can also say 'I'm looking forward to meeting you,' as this is also correct. The only difference between 'I'm looking forward to meeting you' and 'I look forward to meeting you' is that the first one is slightly less formal in tone.
I'm looking forward to never seeing this mistake again!

Use whichever form you like, choosing to use *looking* or *look*, so you can say either 'I look forward to...' or 'I'm looking forward to...,' but please make sure you have the *ing* form after the *to* no matter which form you use!

Look forward to is not the only verb phrase that takes the *ing*. There are several others. I will give examples of the most commonly used ones here, in the interest of ass saving:

'I'm interested in...'
'He's interested in playing the guitar. He started taking lessons last week.'
'My sister has never been interested in traveling.'

'I'm scared of ...'
'I'm scared of hearing strange sounds in the night.'
'His girlfriend was scared of dancing in public, so they just danced in the living room.'

'I'm curious about...'
'I'm curious about hearing the news later today. Will he be found guilty or innocent?'
'She was very curious about baking the tiramisu cheesecake, as she had never done it before.'

Extra vitamins!

Since we are focusing on using the *ing* form, there are several verbs in English where you can use either the *ing* form (walking, talking, going, etc.) or the infinitive (to walk, to talk, to go) after the verb. I will give two examples so you can see how it's used: both of the verbs listed below (to start and to forbid) can take either the *ing* form or the infinitive form after the verb:

'*She started reading* 50 Shades of Grammar *right away.*'
'*She started to read* 50 Shades of Grammar *right away.*'

'*The police forbid us from walking on this bridge, as it is not safe.*'
'*The police forbid us to walk on this bridge, as it is not safe.*'

20. 'IF YOU WANT TO SOUND LIKE A COOL ALIEN, KEEP DOING THIS.'

PROBLEM:
'Greets!' (or the cooler version, 'Greetz!') This is often found at the end of an email or a letter.

DIAGNOSIS:
Every time I see this (daily!) in an email, I give it a perfect 10. Because that's exactly how many toes of mine curl every time I see it. This is from the Dutch ending *groetjes*, and people just translate it literally into English. It does mean greetings; however, what most people fail to realize is that this is used only on a holiday card during Christmastime, and then only with *Season's* before it. You'll see 'Season's Greetings!' all the time on cards between November and January. *Greetings* is also a typical salutation aliens use when they emerge from their UFO on Earth for the first time. They usually say 'Greetings, earthlings!' Is this how you want to sound? Can you ride a bicycle over the moon? I don't think so.

REMEDY:
The reason English people think this is really weird is twofold: 1) they don't know the Dutch word *groetjes*, so have no idea where it's coming from; and 2) if we ever

use *greetings*, it's used at the beginning of a conversation, never at the end. Please stop freaking people out by using this word. Let's talk about other ways to end a letter or email.

In a formal letter, you can end with 'Yours sincerely' or 'Sincerely yours'. 'Yours sincerely' is more American in style, and 'Sincerely yours' is more British. You can also end with 'Yours faithfully' in British English. A good neutral phrase to use is 'Best regards' or a friendlier 'Warm regards', if you know the person you are writing to (and if thoughts about them make you warm). You can also end with 'Best', which is used quite a lot. Try 'Thank you' if you want to end by thanking them, or a neutral 'Sincerely' when you have no idea what else to say. 'Best wishes' is also great when you want to end on a positive note.

For an email, these may seem a bit too formal. There are lots of cool alternatives. You can end with 'Many thanks', 'Take care', 'Adios', 'Cheers', 'Rock on!', and my personal favorite: 'Stay awesome'.

Other great sentences to use before you sign off are:
'Please don't hesitate to contact me if you have any questions.'
'I'm looking forward to hearing from you.'
'Thanks so much for your time.'
'Please let me know if you need anything else.'
'Feel free to mail with any questions or comments you might have.'

Extra Vitamins!

And how do you *start* an email or letter? If you know the person well, just say 'Dear Jane' (if her name is Jane. Otherwise, she might get confused). If you are writing to a man you don't know well, you can say 'Dear Mr. Johnson'. However, if you are writing to a woman, please be aware that there's a difference between *Mrs.* and *Ms.* and *Miss*. People confuse these all the time. *Mrs.* is used when the woman is married and she has taken her husband's surname. Don't use this unless you know that she has taken her husband's name. When I get mail addressed to Mrs. Duberman, I always give it to my mother! *Miss* is used for someone who is clearly unmarried; it is often used for young ladies and girls. However, some women (and other people) feel this is outdated, and might be offended if they are addressed as 'Miss' when they are older and professional. I always tell my clients to go with 'Dear Ms. XXXX' if they are unsure, as that's the most neutral way to express it, and you won't piss anyone off.

Do NOT start a letter or email using the word *Dear* without a name after it, just because in Dutch you can start it with *Beste*. *Dear* is used as a term of endearment. That's like starting your mails with *Schatje*. Is this how you want to address people you don't know? I don't think so, my dear.

You can also use 'To Whom It May Concern' if you don't know who you are addressing, but that's quite formal and becoming a bit old-fashioned thanks to the goodness of the internet. Now it's usually possible to search for the name of the person you want to reach online first. I always recommend doing this because it shows the other person that you have made an effort in finding them.

Oh, and while we're at it...if you are including an attachment, don't say 'Hereby is the attachment'. That word 'hereby' is not often used in general English communication (although, to be honest, it is still occasionally used in formal legal situations – 'I hereby resign as Chief Financial Officer'). Say 'The new document is attached' or 'Please see attachment.'

Ik voelde me een keer heel erg slecht omdat ik een cliënt mailde en eindigde met 'Kont goed!'. Een bijzonder aardig iemand op Twitter antwoordde dat hij eens een Engelse mail had afgesloten met 'Kind retards'. Zucht.

SPELL CHECK YOURSELF BEFORE YOU WRECK YOURSELF
Let me now save your lovely ass, my dear, letter by letter. I have actually read every single one of these mistakes. And laughed. And sometimes cried.

'I am looking for a good English couch – perhaps you can help me?'
Yes. Get a Chesterfield. If you're looking for a good English coach, I know people.

'John Lennon's message was give pies a chance.'
Sigh. I don't think that John Lennon was fighting for the rights of pastries. I really don't. *Pies* (pronounced 'piyz') is the plural of pie – you know, the thing you put apples, cherries, or chocolate in and then eat the whole thing before anyone catches you? Yes. Those are pies. John did say 'Give peace a chance'. *Peace* (pronounced 'pees') is what we need more of in the world, that's for sure. It's the absence of war. But don't confuse that with piece – which sounds exactly the same as peace, but refers to a part or a section of a greater whole – like...a...(feel it coming...) *piece* of something! (See what I did there?) And last, but not least, we also have *peas*. That word is the plural of pea, which is a green vegetable. And I've got a feeling you might have heard of the Black Eyed Peas (see what I did there?) It ends with a slight z sound, as opposed to *peace* which ends in an s sound.

'I am very concerned about the future of the European Onion.'
This person means European *Union*. At least I hope he did! Do I really have to explain what the difference is between an onion and a union? No? Well, thank God for small miracles.

'It's really important to work hard if you want to make it in the music busyness.'
Although people in the music industry work very hard and are busy most of the time, I don't think this person was referring to that. *Busyness* refers to the state of being busy. It's pronounced 'BIZeeness'. *Business* refers to something work-related and is pronounced 'BIZnis'. Glad we cleared that one up.

'Do I pay you in dollars or in Eros?'
Yes, this was mail from a prospective client. I asked to be paid in Eros because I prefer the ancient Greek god of love much more than Euros, which is just a boring currency you can buy stuff with. Give me love gods any day!

'The making off our new video!!'
If I had a dollar for every time I saw this one, I'd be living in a gold-plated mansion with a very attractive stranger feeding me grapes, slowly. *Off* (pronounced 'awff') is the opposite of *on*. It's often used in combination with verbs. For example, *get off* ('Get off that mechanical bull immediately!'), *take off* ('Our plane didn't take off on time because we were waiting for Rihanna'), and *put off* ('Never put off tomorrow what you can do today....or later tonight!'). *Of* (pronounced 'uv') is used to indicate

distance ('I live a mile south of the nearest bingo parlor'), or to show the material or substance of something ('Her "silver" ring was made of tin foil'), or used for questions with *how much* ('How much of a problem will it be if I press this red button?'), or *how long* ('How long of a drive is it to the nearest police station?'). Can you use both in a sentence? Sure you can! I can. 'The making of their new video was so expensive, they had to put off their new English lessons until next year.' But you already knew that.

'My band is so good life – you have to come and see us!'
I hope everyone has a good *life*. Even people who get confused when they spell. I'm sure their *live* shows are great, though! (Oh, and this way of saying *live* is pronounced 'liyv', but you can also say 'liv', which is a verb – 'I live on the second floor.')

'Thank you Buffi for your very helpful advise.'
Actually, darling, I never gave you any advise. I did, however give you lots of *advice*. And some of it was to work on your spelling. I love advising my clients! *Advise* is a verb — it simply means to give *advice* (and *advice* is a noun, but I bet you knew that already, you sexy grammar nerd, you.)

'I am on a diet. I hope to loose three kilos.'
Actually, you don't. You hope to *lose* three kilos (although I think you are beautiful just the way you are). If you lose that weight, I guarantee your clothes will be *loose*!

'Its a problem when people don't listen to each other in the band.'
It's also a problem when people don't check their spelling. We use *its* to show possession ('I have to fix my bike. Its front wheel has somehow mysteriously disappeared.') *It's* is short for 'it is' ('It's too early in the morning to listen to Lady Gaga! Let's put on Motörhead instead!'), or 'it has' ('It's been 7 hours and 15 days since you took your love away.')

'I watched a lot of video's on vacation.'
I see this kind of mistake a lot. Watch out – we don't use *s* after a word unless it means possession ('My dog's new Halloween costume is da bomb!'). If you mean to use it to represent something plural, just add *s* at the end of the word. *Videos, films, movies, etc.* All good. Which brings me to another classic:

'My brothers' band is so awesome!'
I know who wrote this, and I know she has only one brother who plays in a band. She should have said 'my *brother's* band', because it, the band, belongs to her (one) brother. However, if the word is plural, then you can use *s'* after the word to show possession – 'The *brothers'* alibi gave them away as the Rodeo Clown Mafia immediately.'

'Your welcome!'
My welcome what? My welcome mat? If you say *your*, you mean belonging to you ('Your hot air balloon got stuck in my tree again.'). If you say *you're*, you mean 'you are' ('You're the wind beneath my wings.'). Which is what I was. Welcome. Welcome to Spelling Disaster Land!

'I'm going to talk to my manager, than I will let you know.'
We use *than* to talk about comparison: 'That Ferrari is more expensive than I thought!' Use *then* for talking about time: 'First I make my organic decaf soy latte, then I scramble my tofu.'

DON'T GO THERE!

'I had a girlfriend last year but I made it out.'
I think you mean you broke up with her. You can make out with your girlfriend, but I don't think I should really go there.

'I am coming at home later today.'
This one is a classic. If you are coming AT home, this means that you are having your orgasm at home later that day. I'm so glad you shared that information with me. Even better, sometimes I hear 'I'm not coming at home today,' which makes me think 'Oh? Where will you be having your orgasm today, then?' Don't go there. Just say 'I'm coming/not coming home', without the *at*. Two little letters can make your coach blush.

'That news is not actual anymore.'
Actual in English means not fake: 'Is that an actual diamond? Are you actually engaged? This person meant 'current' when they used 'actual'. They should have said the news is out of date or no longer relevant.

'Sorry I'm late, the files were terrible this morning.'
You mean traffic, right? Or were you abducted by aliens who shrunk you to the size of a pea and put you in a huge filing cabinet and you couldn't find your way out? Is that why you're late? No. I didn't think so either.

'I have a special Buffi map for all my assignments.'
That's lovely. I am honored that you view me as a country that you want to discover and learn more about. However, I'm pretty much an open book, so you don't really need a map. What you do need is to write this correction down in your Buffi file. Thanks!

'My computer, he is broken.'
'Does your computer have a penis?'
'No.'
'Then it's not a he.'
'Oh. My computer, she is broken.'
In English we refer to something as *he* or *she* if we know that it has either male or female parts. Otherwise, use *it*. (We do sometimes refer to a ship as *she*, however.)

'Let me explain you the situation.'
Thank you my dear, but you don't really have to explain me. I know about me...or does this relate to the 'Buffi map' you referred to earlier? I'd love it if you explained the situation TO me, though.

'My sister-in-law got really drunk and started a fight – that's so typical!'
In English, the word *typical* means something that's usual or normal, or defines the person or situation. In Dutch, it's the opposite. So either you're telling me that your sister-in-law is an alcoholic bully, or that she acted in a very unusual way. I hope it's the latter!

'So great to see you again! How do you do?'
How do I do...my laundry? The dishes? Oh, you mean 'How are you?', right? Because we only use 'How do you do?' for the first time we meet someone, and never again after that. But you knew that, and just forgot, right?

'She's in a meeting on the moment.'
I'm grateful you said *in* a meeting, because that's the right preposition to use. However, it's *at* the moment when you're talking about time. Or maybe you meant that your boss is in a meeting on, or about, 'the moment'? Sigh. I've never had a meeting about 'the moment'. What am I doing wrong with my life?!?

CHAPTER 3

GRAMMAR GRIEF

Oh, darling, you're nearly there! I have saved the best part for last in this section, at least if you are a Grammar Goddess like me! I hope now you have an idea of just how complicatedly interesting English can be. And that's before we even tackle these beauties. This section covers common mistakes made in the basic tenses, and mistakes stemming from adjectives, adverbs, comparisons, question tags, prepositions, and phrasal verbs, just to name a few. Warning: this section is not for the weak-hearted. You might want to consult with a medical professional before diving deep into the cold and murky waters of Grammatical Theory. Let's drown together.

My *Don't Go There* list will put a smile on your face and a song in your heart – it will make you realize that there are people out there who speak English worse than you do.

21. 'NO HORSEHEAD IN THE BED, I BEG OF YOU!'

PROBLEM:
'I do work in Rotterdam.'

DIAGNOSIS:
This person is trying to tell us that he works in Rotterdam. Which is a lovely thing to know. However, if you use *do* for a statement ('I do work...'), it usually means that you want to make something absolutely clear. It's often used during an argument or to clear up a misunderstanding: 'I do live in Amsterdam, I really do! I swear I don't live in that bordello in Brussels!' If you say, 'I do work in Rotterdam' as part of a normal conversation (as many of you do, but I still love you), it could be interpreted as being aggressive, threatening, or quite defensive. Your listeners might think you are a member of the mafia, and will live in fear of waking up with a horsehead in their bed in the morning. Don't go there. Unless, of course, you are actually a gangster, in which case I'd like to say that you do look lovely today.

SECTION ONE   71

REMEDY:

Use *do* for questions, not for statements. For example, 'Do you work in Rotterdam?' An appropriate answer would be 'Yes, I do.' (if you do work there; otherwise an appropriate answer would be 'No, I don't.')

We use *do* for I, you, we, and they, and *does* for he, she, and it. When asking a question, don't forget to use *do* and *does* plus the original verb (work, talk, go, etc.):

'Does she live in New York? I thought she moved to Boston.'
'Do you live near the train station? Could you pick me up?'
'Do we have to go to the Bible Ballet Opera tonight? I'm still recovering from the last time we went.'

THE MAGIC *S*

'Where does she works?' is geen goede zin. Het moet zijn: 'Where does she work?' Een makkelijke manier om dit te onthouden? *Got one!* Does eindigt met een *s*, en omdat daar dan al een *s* in zit, heeft het werkwoord dat erop volgt geen *s* meer nodig. Hier moet je gewoon het oorspronkelijke werkwoord gebruiken:
'*Does she work in Utrecht?*'
'*Does he like chocolate covered crickets?*'

Je kunt deze vragen beantwoorden met 'Yes, she does' of 'Yes, he does.' Dezelfde regel gaat op voor de negatieve vorm van *does*, *doesn't*:
'*She doesn't work in Utrecht.*'
'*He doesn't like chocolate covered crickets.*'

Extra vitamins!

Let's focus on formulating questions for a moment. We have many ways of asking a question in English. If you want more than a yes or a no as an answer, start with a 'question word' like where, when, why, how, how much, how often, how many. what, etc. As far as word order goes, these words always go before the *do* or *does* in a question:

'Where do you live?'
'Why do you live there?'
'How often does she get her hair cut?'
'When does he take out the garbage? It smells like it's been a while!'

'I live in Utrecht ' or 'I'm living in Utrecht?'

PRESENT SIMPLE
If you use the verb (werkwoord) without the *ing* form ('I live', 'she goes', 'we study', etc.) , it's the *present simple* form. This is used for things that happen on a regular basis – things you do every week, month, or year. It's used to describe permanent situations, things you don't expect to end or change:
'I take a hot yoga class every week – I love getting sweaty with strangers!'
'She gets a new tattoo every year, and every year they get worse.'
'Every Sunday, he goes out for dinner at his favorite kosher Korean restaurant.'

PRESENT CONTINUOUS
The verb + *ing* form (also known as *present continuous* tense or *present progressive* tense) is used for things happening at this moment, or for things you expect to end or change. It's used to describe temporary situations or activities:
'I'm having an excellent lunch now – care to join me? The fried monkey brains are just divine!'
'She is living in Barcelona for two months to rock her bullfighting skills.'

HOE GEEF JE OP EEN SUBTIELE MANIER KRITIEK?
We gebruiken *always* + werkwoord + *ing* om kritiek te geven, of om irritatie of frustratie te tonen. Wanneer het al de hele week heeft geregend, zou ik naar buiten kunnen kijken en kunnen zeggen 'It's *always raining* in Holland.' (Of course, this situation is completely hypothetical.) Wanneer iemand rookt in de auto zou je kunnen zeggen: 'You're *always* smoking when you drive – do you know how bad that is?'

SECTION TWO   73

GOOD NEWS OR BAD NEWS?

Keep good news permanent by using the *present simple* form: 'We produce high-quality products.' If you use the *present continuous* form – 'We're producing high-quality products' – then it sounds like 'Oh! Our products normally suck but today something magical happened and wow! High quality! Grab your chance because it won't last long!' If you say, 'My team is working really hard' it could be interpreted that you really mean 'I work with the laziest bunch of losers you have ever seen.' If you have bad news, keep it temporary, which means using the *ing* form of the verb. If you say, 'We have problems with our website' then it means that your website stinks 24/7. However, if you say, 'We are having problems with our website', that tells me three things: 1) You have identified a problem; 2) You are working on it; and 3) It will be resolved soon. Use the language to your advantage, especially in professional communication!

Gebruik nooit *do + ing* of *does + ing*! 'Where does she going?' Ik hoor dit véél te vaak. Het moet zijn: 'Where *is* she going?'

22. 'NOW YOU…KNOW.'

PROBLEM:
'I didn't knew the answer.'

DIAGNOSIS:
I heard 'I didn't knew…' but I'm sure this person meant 'I didn't know…' I'm sure that's what they meant. That's what they meant, right? Because after the word *did* or *didn't* you always use the infinitive form of the verb. So 'I didn't know' is the right way to say this. But maybe they forgot this because they were so distracted by my extremely high IQ. Yeah, that's it.

REMEDY:
The past simple tense is used to talk about things that are finished, over, or history. To make a verb negative in the past simple tense, we use didn't + the original form of the verb:

'I didn't go to the mascara demonstration because I had other plans.'
'She didn't find her keys until she looked in her back pocket.'

To make a question in the *past simple* tense, we use *did* + the original verb.
'Did you buy a Ferrari yesterday? For me?'
'Did Gordon grow a beard? Wow!'

However, to make a positive statement, we need to know first if the verb is *regular* or *irregular*. Watch out for the difference between 'regular' and 'irregular' verbs.

Regular verbs end in *ed*:
'She walked home yesterday.'
'They talked for hours on Skype.'
'He studied Russian for three years before he gave up.'

Irregular verbs...don't. There is no real logic as to why it's:

choose ⟶ chose
have ⟶ had
speak ⟶ spoke
take ⟶ took

so I just suggest you memorize them.

However, there is good news here, and I'm thrilled to share it with you. After the words *did* and *didn't*, we always use the infinitive form of the verb (to walk, to go, to talk, etc.). Here you don't even need to think about the issue of the verb being regular or irregular. Just use *did* or *didn't* and the infinitive, and you're good to go!
'I didn't get home until 9 P.M. last night.'
'Sparkles, the rodeo clown, didn't realize the angry bull was in the ring until it was too late.'
'Did you finish that report on time?'

You only need to worry about the *irregular* form of the verb during a positive statement:
'I got home at 9.'
'She left the party on time.'
'He saw the bull too late.'

SAY IT LIKE YOU MEAN IT!

Watch out! Alleen maar omdat een werkwoord regelmatig (regular) is, en eindigt op *ed*, betekent het nog niet dat je al precies weet hoe je het moet uitspreken. Soms eindigt het met een t-klank, probeer deze woorden maar eens: *walked, worked,* en *talked*. Het kan ook eindigen op een d-klank – *smelled, pulled,* en *hugged*. En, *just to keep things interesting*, het kan ook eindigen met een id-klank: *waited, visited,* en *decided* bijvoorbeeld.

WE BELIEVE YOU!

Wanneer je *did* gebruikt voor een positief statement, betekent het dat je een punt wilt benadrukken. Je doet dit bijvoorbeeld wanneer je een discussie hebt met iemand of wanneer je een misverstand uit de weg wilt helpen:
'I did *go on vacation last year.*'
'She did *study English for a long time.*'
'They did *work on that top-secret project.*'

Wanneer je het echter niet zo bedoelt klinkt het vrij defensief, net zoals wanneer je *do* gebruikt in een positief statement – 'I *do* live in Rotterdam' – zie punt **21** op pagina 70 voor meer informatie over deze vorm.

Extra vitamins!

The rule is, if you have a question or a negative in the past simple, you use *did* or *didn't*. We know that now. However, if your verb is *to be*, then we have a different rule for this. *To be* is, as I've said before, a freak in the grammar circus – it has its own set of rules. The past form of *to be* is 'was' (for I, he, she, it) and 'were' (for you, we, they). If we were to follow the normal rule, we would say things like 'Did you be at the party last night?' Or 'She didn't be on vacation last week.' Doesn't that sound weird? If this sounds normal to you, then you've been hanging out with the wrong kind of people. The right way to say this is 'Were you at the party last night?' and 'She wasn't on vacation last week.' The negative form of *to be* is 'wasn't' or 'weren't' and the question form is 'was' or 'were'. We don't say *didn't be* in English. Ever. So don't go there, darling! Thank you.

23. BAD GRAMMAR CAN KILL!

PROBLEM:
'I *have seen* that yesterday.'

DIAGNOSIS:
This is a literal translation of 'Ik heb dat gisteren gezien.' Many people translate *heb gezien* or *heb gedaan*, etc., to have seen and have done. However, this form, 'I have seen' (called the *present perfect*) is used differently in English: it is used for situations or actions that have not finished yet.

The correct way to say the sentence above is 'I *saw* that yesterday.' Why? I'm glad you asked! The time period – yesterday – is finished; therefore you should use the *past simple* (was, were, went, saw, etc.). The *present perfect* is used for situations that are not finished. If you say 'I *have never* met my uncle,' this means that he lives far away, or your paths have not crossed yet, but you can still meet him in the future. However, if you say, 'I never *met* my uncle', then your uncle is dead and you will never get the chance to meet him. Bad grammar can kill, people!

REMEDY:
In English we have several different forms of the past, and each one tells its own story. The purpose of this book is not to dive too deep into the chilly waters of grammatical theory, but allow me to break down some basic forms for you here, in the interest of ass saving. When using the past tense (verleden tijd), you need to think about the situation you are describing – is the situation (or time period) finished or not finished?

Past Progressive
If you are focusing on a specific moment in a period of time that is finished, use the *past progressive* (*was* or *were* + the verb + *ing*):
'I *was getting* tattooed at 4.30 this afternoon.'
'She *was running* to the bus when she tripped and fell and lost her gold tooth.'
'I'm sorry I didn't answer when you called. We *were skinny dipping* with friends last night.'

Present Perfect

As I mentioned before, if the situation or time period is still continuing (such as this week, this month, this year, or today), then you need to use the *present perfect* (have gone, has seen, have studied, has worked, etc.):

'*I have had 18 cups of tea today.*'
'*He has been to Scotland twice this year. He looks so good in a kilt!*'
'*Have you ever been to the opera?*'

DE BATTERIJMETAFOOR

Zoals je weet is 'I didn't went' en 'I didn't knew' fout. Ja, altijd. *Did* staat al in verleden tijd, waardoor je niet ook nog eens het hele werkwoord in de verleden tijd moet plaatsen. Ik leer mijn studenten en cliënten altijd om aan een batterij te denken wanneer ze het even niet meer weten. Ik weet dat dit heel raar klinkt, maar het helpt, echt waar. Een batterij werkt alleen met een positieve en een negatieve kant. Wanneer er twee positieve of twee negatieve kanten zijn zullen je afstandsbediening of kookwekker het vermoedelijk niet doen. Probeer dit te visualiseren en pas het toe op de *past simple*. Wanneer het eerste werkwoord in een zin in de verleden tijd staat (bijvoorbeeld *did*), dan moet het volgende werkwoord in de tegenwoordige tijd staan (*go, know*, etc.). *Didn't went* werkt niet omdat er twee keer achter elkaar verleden tijd wordt gebruikt. Deze regel gaat ook op voor de *present perfect*: als je begint met *has* of *have*' (beide in tegenwoordige tijd) dan gebruik je daarna de participle form – *been, gone, lived*, etc., om te laten zien dat het in het verleden plaatsvindt. *I hope my crazy battery metaphor gives you extra energy for the rest of this section!*

24. 'TAKE ME TO VEGAS, BABY!'

PROBLEM:
'When I win the lottery, I will buy a new car.'

DIAGNOSIS:
I'm not sure, but I think this person has confused *when* and *if*. She doesn't know for sure that she will win the lottery, so she should have used *if*. Unless, of course,

she is a Dutch medium and has special psychic powers that enable her to see into and control the future. Then I want her to take me to Vegas – we'll make the Rain Man look like an amateur!

Now let's get back to business. *If* expresses a hypothetical possibility. This means it is used when you are not sure if something is going to happen or not:
'If it rains, I will have to cancel our picnic.'
'If he asks me to marry him, I will have to say no, because I am already engaged to Justin Bieber.'
'If they increase their prices, we will be forced to terminate the contract.'

When is used for situations that are certain, although you might not know exactly when it will happen:
'When I win the lottery, I always buy a bottle of champagne to celebrate.'
'When it rains, you get wet.'
'When they increase their prices, we will announce it to the media.'

REMEDY:
If you are unsure about something happening, use *if*. If you are certain about something happening, use *when*.

Extra vitamins!

I was just pretty sneaky and introduced the concept of conditionals without you realizing it (if you knew this, Grammar Nerd High Five!). Say what, mama? A conditional? What's that? I am so glad you asked, darling! A conditional is a fancy way of expressing a hypothetical situation (using the word *if*), and its consequence. We have three types of conditionals, and I will give you a simple explanation of each one to maintain the ass-saving journey that you have joined me on. We will go more into detail on how these are effective in business English in chapter 5.

Basically, Type 1 is used for situations that could actually happen in the future. Type 2 is used to express doubt or to give advice, and Type 3 is used to look back on situations that are too late to change.

Conditional Type 1
This type of structure is used for situations that could actually happen. It's easiest if you remember this as a simple formula. Here it is:

If + present simple –> will/may/can + rest of the sentence.

'If it rains, I will cancel our naked karaoke contest.'
'If it snows, I will go skiing.'
'If you work hard, you can do well at school.'
'If you don't have a driver's license, you may not drive.'

Notice how the *will* is not used in the same part of the sentence as the *if*? Always keep them separate. The *if* and the *will*, *may*, or *can* are never in the same part of the sentence. 'If it *will* rain, we will cancel our naked karaoke contest' is wrong.

Conditional Type 2
This is used to express doubt, or for giving advice. The magic formula for this is listed below.

If + past simple –> would/might/could + the rest of the sentence.

Look closely at the following sentences. Can you feel that a sense of doubt has now entered the situation?
'If it *snowed*, I *would* go skiing.' (This sounds like this person wants to go skiing but it's not snowing yet!)
'If you *worked* hard, you *could* do well at school.' (But you're a lazy pig so I hope you haven't chosen a graduation dress yet.)

Conditional Type 2 is also used for giving advice. We usually start with 'If I were you, I would...':
'If I were you, I wouldn't buy Buffi that Mercedes. I would buy her that orange Ferarri instead.'
'If I were you, I'd grab Lowlands tickets as fast as possible – it's going to sell out fast!'

Notice how we use 'I were' in the last two sentences? Isn't that freaky? We never use 'I were' in any other situation. Check this: 'I were so tired yesterday.' Doesn't that sound weird? It should. We only use 'I were' in the construction 'If I were you...' It's called the subjunctive. Just wanted to share that with the group.

Conditional Type 3

Conditional Type 3 is quite different from Type 1 (looking ahead and being realistic) and Type 2 (looking ahead and being doubtful, or giving advice). Type 3 actually looks back. It looks back on a situation that is too late to change. It can be used for positive or negative situations. The complicated formula (you can handle it, honey!) for this one is as follows:

If + had + past participle –> would have/could have/should have + past participle

'If he had worn a seatbelt, he would have survived the accident.'
'If she had found that ticket sooner, she would have realized she won the lottery!'
'If I had known you needed that report done by Friday, I would have had it finished on time!'

Conditionals 1, 2, and 3 in action

Let's see all three conditionals in action. If you've applied for a job and you have a really good feeling about it after your interview, you might say:
'If they are interested, they'll call me!'
(*Type 1* – looking ahead, realistic chance of happening).

Two weeks go by (sloooooowly) and you haven't heard anything yet. Then you could say:
'If they were interested, they would call me!'
(*Type 2* – doubtful situation).

You hear that they hired your ex-girlfriend for the job instead (beyotch!). You hang your head in sorrow and say:
'If they had been interested, they would have hired me!'
(*Type 3*, looking back, too late to change).

25. 'ARE YOU SPIDERMAN?'

PROBLEM:
'I learned it *on school*.'

DIAGNOSIS:
On is a *preposition* (like *in, at, over, under, before*, etc.) We have prepositions of time, place, and movement. Many people literally translate prepositions from one language to another. In Dutch, you say 'op school', so it makes sense to think that 'on school' would be the same in English. However, it's not. If you say 'on school', you are talking about the surface of the building. This could be the walls or the roof of the school. I don't know anyone who could be on school, except for Spiderman (or maybe Sinterklaas).

REMEDY:
Let's look at the prepositions *in, on,* and *at* when they are used as prepositions of place. When you think 'on school', think of Spiderman first. If this is not you, then say 'at school'. *At* is the preposition we use when talking about *location*. I call it the cell phone preposition. When people call each other and ask 'Where are you?', the answer is usually formed with *at* – 'I'm at the office,' 'at work', 'at school', 'at the dentist', etc.

We would use *on*, as I said earlier, to describe the surface of something. The spider (and maybe the man!) can be on the ceiling, the painting can be on the wall, there can be carpet on the floor, and there can be a superhero (or a chimney! Or both!) on the roof. I often hear that people are 'on' a festival, but this is not correct. Not even for Spiderman. We're all *at* a festival.

And what about *in*, you may wonder? I'm so glad you asked! *In* can be thought of as short for inside. So when you are surrounded by something, you can use *in*:
'I'm in the restaurant having a nice lunch.'
'There was a fire in that old church and it burned down years ago.'
'I had a great time in New York last summer!'

Watch out! If you say to someone 'I'll meet you at the restaurant,' chances are they will be waiting for you outside the restaurant. If you say 'I'll meet you in the restaurant,' they might be at the table already waiting for you. I wouldn't want you to miss out on a great dinner date! Using the wrong preposition can leave you lost and lonely. And hungry!

'AT SCHOOL' OF 'IN SCHOOL'?

Ik krijg vaak de vraag wat het verschil is tussen 'at school' en 'in school'. Eigenlijk is er maar een klein verschil. Wanneer we zeggen dat iemand 'in school' is, betekent dat vaak dat iemand zich op dat moment *in* het klaslokaal bevindt. 'At school' is veel breder: iemand bevindt zich dan in ieder geval in de buurt van de school. Je zou bijvoorbeeld kunnen zeggen: 'There was a football match *at school* on Saturday but nobody was *in school* at the time.' Of: 'He's not here; he's *at school* now, but I don't know which classroom he is *in* at the moment.'

Time to check out...

Prepositions of Time

Many people get confused when it comes to prepositions of time. It's actually pretty simple. *At* is used to describe the time on the clock – at noon, at midnight, at lunchtime, at 4.56 P.M. (Check back to sections 2 and 3 for more information on time.) *On* is used for days of the week: on Monday, on Tuesday, etc. It's also used for other special days: 'on my birthday', 'On Easter Sunday', 'On Christmas morning', etc.

In is used for longer periods of time – in the morning, in the afternoon, in the evening (but *at* night!), in the summer, in the future, in the Dark Ages, etc. If you have the day of the week first, you have to use *on* and not *in* – for example, we say 'in the morning' but 'on Monday morning', 'in the afternoon' but 'on Monday afternoon', 'in the evening' but 'on Monday evening', and 'at night' but 'on Monday night'.

DON'T LIKE PREPOSITIONS?

Wanneer je de woorden *this, next, last* of *every* gebruikt, heb je geen voorzetsel meer nodig:
'Every Tuesday afternoon I go to my Bingo Anonymous group.'
'Next Wednesday morning I will finally get my scrapbooking diploma.'
'Last Friday night we danced on tabletops and we drank too many shots.'
'This Thursday evening I am having some friends over for our annual Naked Twister competition.'

Now, darling, it's time to move on to the last group of prepositions for now...

Prepositions of Movement
Just a few words about prepositions of movement, as people sometimes mix these up. If you want to talk about movement with a specific destination, use *to*:
'He walked to the pub to buy an attractive stranger a beer.'
'She moved to Berlin in 2012 to improve her hipster skills.'
'Sid is not here; he's gone to the shops to buy Nancy some flowers.'

If you want to talk about movement from one side of an enclosed space to the other side, use *through*:
'The train went through the tunnel and created a lot of noise.'
'He walked through the building to make sure all the windows were closed.'

To talk about movement from one side of a surface to another, use *across*:
'She ran across the sun-dappled fields into the outstretched arms of her lover...in the granola commercial.'
'He swam across the canal to save the drowning kitten and won the Cool Cat Award last year.'

26. 'YOU NEED ME. MORE THAN YOU THINK!'

PROBLEM:
'I don't need your lessons, Buffi, because I speak English very good.' (Yes, I heard this.)

DIAGNOSIS:

This person has made two critical mistakes. One is that they have used *good* to describe an action, instead of using *well*. The other mistake is that he thought he could live without me. Ha!

REMEDY:

This person should have said, 'I speak English well.' (I mean, if it were true.) *Good* is an *adjective (bijvoeglijk naamwoord)*. This means that it describes *nouns (zelfstandig naamwoorden)* – people, places, and things, as in the examples below:
'She is a really good cook, we should check out her new vegan steakhouse one day!'
'Los Angeles is a good city to live in, if you love traffic.'
'That is such a good book you're reading – the butler did it, just so you know.'

Just as in Dutch, adjectives can also come before the *noun* or *pronoun (voornaamwoord)* – like he, she, or it, for example – or after it: 'That is such a cute puppy!' or 'That puppy is so cute!' Both sentences are correct. *Well* is an *adverb (bijwoord)* and is used to describe actions. Adverbs usually answer the question *how*, *when*, or *where* something happens. You can say:
'She did really well – she passed all her exams!'
'He sang so well at his concert, he gave two extra encores!'
'She didn't drive very well, so she didn't pass her driver's test.'

Luckily, most adjectives and adverbs are nearly the same. They are separated by only two letters. Most adverbs end with *ly*. If *slow* is the adjective, then *slowly* is the adverb:
'My grandmother is such a slow driver.'
'She always drives so slowly when passing cute construction workers.'

If *beautiful* is the adjective, then *beautifully* is the adverb:
'That is such a beautiful painting.'
'She painted her nails beautifully before going to the rodeo.'

We gebruiken *well* ook wel in bepaalde beschrijvende uitdrukkingen. Je kunt bijvoorbeeld zeggen dat iemand *well-dressed* is, *well-educated* of *well-mannered*. We zeggen ook 'Well done!' wanneer we vinden dat iemand iets heel goed heeft gedaan, of wanneer ons wordt gevraagd hoe we onze biefstuk willen. *Got it, darling? Well done!*

Extra vitamins!

Watch out! Not all adverbs end with *ly*. We have just seen *well* as an example, because *goodly* sounds freaky – just use *well* instead. The word *fast* is an adjective and an adverb:
'She drove the car fast to get away from the police.'
'Her fast driving skills impressed the policeman, who fell in love with her instantly.'

My little quick and dirty tip for this one is if you are in doubt about whether to say *quick* or *quickly*, just say *fast* and you're good to go!

Got it, darling? Are you with me so far? Excellent, because now I'm about to throw you a curveball. We also have some *adjectives* that end in *ly* – for example, *elderly, lovely,* and *lonely*:
'Her elderly aunt had to move to a nursing home.'
'That's such a lovely reindeer sweater – and who says you can't wear that at Easter?'
'She felt so lonely when her blind date never showed up for disco bowling.'

Use your senses! If you are describing something related to the senses – how something tastes, feels, smells, etc. – don't use the adverb form, use the adjective. 'This coffee tastes well' is not correct. In this sentence, you are describing how the coffee tastes. However, because the coffee doesn't have a mouth and is unable to taste anything, you need to use the adjective form: 'This coffee tastes good.' If you say 'this shampoo smells well', a native English speaker might think that bottle of shampoo has a functioning nose floating in it (um...gross!). Don't go there. You can say 'You smell good' when someone is wearing a lovely cologne or perfume: 'You smell so good – are you wearing Buffi's new fragrance, Eau de la Grammaire'?

You can say 'You smell well' when you are talking about their smelling skills. Here you are describing how someone uses their ability to smell: 'You smell pretty well for someone who has a terrible cold! I had no idea that milk was spoiled!'

LOOK OUT!

We know now that *to look* can describe how someone appears. We use the *adjective form* with this:
She looked angry.
He looked tired yesterday after riding that mechanical bull for an hour.
They looked hungry at the end of their mountain climbing class.

Deze zinnen beschrijven hoe iemand eruit ziet, daarom wordt het bijvoeglijk naamwoord (adjective) gebruikt. Echter, wanneer je het voorzetsel 'at' toevoegt, bijvoorbeeld *to look at*, creëer je een actie, waardoor het bijvoeglijk naamwoord verandert in een bijwoord (adverb), de *ly* vorm.
She looked at the baby angrily when it tried to bite her nose ring.
He looked at her tiredly and said: 'It's your turn to ride the mechanical bull.'
They looked at the tofu hungrily, as it had been at least two hours since their last soy meal.

Viel de verandering in spelling je op? Angry veranderde in *angrily*, hungry veranderde in *hungrily*. En dan nog iets: wanneer het bijvoeglijk naamwoord (adjective) eindigt op een e, verdwijnt deze in de bijwoordvorm:
He is a terrible dancer.
He danced terribly at the party.
She is a horrible dresser.
She dressed so horribly she was kicked out of the fashion show!

27. HARDLY WORKING? AHA...SO HOW WAS *EXTREME COUPONING MAKEOVERS WITH THE STARS...ON ICE?*'

PROBLEM:
'I was working so hardly last night!'

DIAGNOSIS:
This person probably meant to say that they were 'working hard' last night (either that or they were actually proud of winning the gold medal in the Couch Potato Olympics).

REMEDY:
This person meant well when they said *hardly* because they were thinking 'I am describing an action, so I should use the adverb form, which ends in *ly*.' (I know that people think about grammar all the time, right?) This works for adverbs (bijwoorden) like *quickly, slowly, carefully*, and *beautifully*. However, it doesn't work for *hard*. The adverb form is *hard*, and so is the adjective form (de bijvoeglijke vorm). So you can say 'Her pole dancing lesson was really hard' or 'She worked really hard to pass her pole dancing test.'

Extra vitamins!

'Hard is an adjective (bijvoeglijk naamwoord). We say *hard, harder,* and *hardest* to talk about degrees of how hard something is. *Beautiful* is also an adjective, but we don't say *beautifuller* and *beautifullest*. So how do we compare adjectives? Why do we say *cheap/cheaper/cheapest* but *expensive/more expensive/most expensive*? Well, as a coach, it's too easy for me to tell you why. I will give you two lists of adjectives, and let's see if you can figure out a pattern:

nice / nicer / nicest
big / bigger / biggest
long / longer / longest
great / greater / greatest
ugly / uglier / ugliest
fancy / fancier / fanciest

beautiful / more beautiful / most beautiful
expensive / more expensive / most expensive
attractive / more attractive / most attractive
fabulous / more fabulous / most fabulous

Can you see why some adjectives end in *er* and *est* and others use *more* and *most*? What did you say? 'It has to do with how long the word is'? By golly, you're right! You hit the nail right on the head. Well done! If a word has one or two syllables (lettergrepen) then we end it in *er* or *est*. If there are three or more, then we use *more* or *most* for comparisons. We do this to stop words from becoming too long in English (although obviously that's not an issue in Dutch).

This was the most beautiful moment in my life, sharing this golden nugget of knowledge with you, dear reader, because you are the kindest person on the planet. (See what I did there?)

We weten nu dat er een groot verschil is tussen *hard* en *hardly*. Wist je dat er ook een verschil is tussen *late* en *lately*?

Late betekent 'niet op tijd', het tegenovergestelde van vroeg:
'*He was* late *to his meeting.*'
'*His meeting started* late.'

Lately betekent recent, niet zo lang geleden:
'*I haven't seen a good movie lately. Can you recommend anything?*'
'*Lately, I've been brushing up on my scrapbooking skills – there's a competition coming up soon, and I want to win the Golden Needle Award!*'

28. 'DO THIS IF YOU WANT TO START A FIGHT.'

PROBLEM:
'Is the car of my brother broken or not?'

DIAGNOSIS:
This lovely person is having trouble expressing a couple of things. Instead of saying 'the car of my brother', he should have known that the correct way to say this is 'my brother's car'. The apostrophe plus *s* shows possession. He also should

not have ended his question with 'or not', because that sounds really threatening and kind of scares me. He should have said 'or isn't it?' However, perhaps he likes frightening women who are much taller than he is.

REMEDY:

When referring to something belonging to someone else, you can say 'my sister's house', 'my dad's mascara', 'my neighbor's wife', etc. If something belongs to you, you can say 'it's mine'. If it belongs to someone else, you can say it's *yours, his, hers, ours,* or *theirs*. For example, if you hear 'Whose coat is this?', you can simply answer 'It's mine.' However, you can also say 'That coat is mine.' If you use the subject of the sentence, then you can say 'It's my coat' or 'It's his coat', 'It's her coat', 'It's our coat', 'It's their coat', or 'It's your coat – don't you remember, you idiot?'

Many Dutch people end their sentences with 'or not?'. This is not a common way of communicating in English, unless you are very angry and need an answer immediately, otherwise someone might get shot. However, we do have a way of checking for agreement or confirmation. We end sentences like this:

'It's a lovely day, isn't it?'
'She's your sister, isn't she?'
'He'll win the election, won't he?'

If you look carefully at the sentences above you'll see that the verbs above are used in the positive form (it is, she is, he will), and the endings are in the negative form (isn't, won't). We can also flip it around, and have a negative verb followed by a positive question at the end of the sentence:

'It's not raining outside, is it?'
'She's not your sister, is she?'
'He won't win the election, will he?'

Can you see why 'or not' sounds a bit too aggressive in English? You can, can't you?

Extra vitamins!

There's a big difference between *who's* and *whose*. They get mixed up all the time, even by native speakers. *Whose* is used when you are asking about something belonging to someone:
'Whose jacket is this? Because I tried it on and it looks great on me!'
'Whose shoes are these? Yours? Can I have them when you die?'
'Whose book is lying on the bed? It's certainly not mine – I would never read the Kama Sutra!'

Who's is short for 'who is':
'Who's coming to our naked picnic next week?'
'Who's your daddy?'
'Who's the one who can make you happy?'

Glad we cleared that up.

Je kunt niet zeggen: 'It's mine book.' Correct is: 'It's my book.' Hetzelfde geldt voor: 'Those are ours chairs.' De juiste vorm is 'Those are our chairs.'. En je weet vast ook dat 'yours movie' niet klopt, toch? Het gekke is echter dat deze regels totaal niet opgaan voor *his* dat kan je op allebei de manieren zeggen:
That book is his.
That's his book.

Isn't that good to know? Let wel een beetje op met het woord *of*: 'a friend of *mine*' is correct, 'a friend of *me*' niet. 'She had drinks with some friends of *yours* last night and found out about your secret One Direction tattoo' is correct; 'She had drinks with some friends of *you*' niet.

29. 'IT'S ALL IN THE WRIST!'

PROBLEM:
'I am an excellent guitarist because I have been playing with myself since I was six.'

DIAGNOSIS:
This is a classic! I actually saw this in an artist's biography. This sentence should, of course, have read, '...because I have been playing since I was six.' 'Playing with myself' means masturbating in English. I'm so happy I saw it before anyone else did, and corrected it right away! Unless, of course, this person actually is proud of the fact that he has been masturbating since the age of six, which has contributed to his excellent guitar-playing skills. Hmmmm...not going there.

REMEDY:
In English we don't have many reflexive verbs. 'Say what, mama?!' 'What's a *reflexive verb* (wederkerend werkwoord)?' you may be thinking. Here's the shizzle. To keep it simple, a reflexive verb is a verb that uses a *reflexive pronoun* (wederkerend voornaamwoord) after it. Reflexive pronouns are *myself, yourself, himself, herself, itself, ourselves,* and *themselves.* Here are a few examples of reflexive verbs used in English. As I said before, we don't have many, so enjoy these rare specimens!

to hurt yourself – '*He hurt himself during the pole-dancing competition.*'
to enjoy yourself – '*She really enjoyed herself on holiday, taking advantage of the all-you-can-eat tofu buffet.*'
to market yourself – '*My manager told me that I should market myself more as a Supermilf and less as a bitchy coach.*'
to deny yourself – '*I hope you never deny yourself the pleasure of using excellent grammar!*'

Extra vitamins!

In English, it sounds pretty lame if you say, 'I dressed myself this morning.' You are allowed to say this until approximately the age of three. After that, you really should be able to dress yourself. If you are a 45-year-old man who rushes up to me and says, 'Sorry I'm late, I had to dress myself in a hurry this morning' (and yes, I have heard this several times), then I will think 'OMG, your poor mother. She must be soooo tired.' In English, we just 'get dressed.'

> 'Getting dressed up' is iets wat je doet voor een feestje – het betekent dat je je mooiste kleren aandoet en je best doet er mooi uit te zien. 'Dressing down' kan ook: dat betekent dat je casual kleren draagt.

The same thing goes for 'shaving myself'. You can say 'I shaved myself today' if you are a barber and have spent the whole day shaving other people and you finally get the chance to shave yourself. If you are not a professional barber in this situation, just 'shave'. Oh, and by the way, speaking of shaving, many people have asked me if I can also shave their ass while I'm saving it. Sorry. For ass shaving you'll have to ask someone else. Thanks.

30. 'HOW TO GIVE ME A HEART ATTACK.'

PROBLEM:
'I will be spending the weekend looking for my children.'

DIAGNOSIS:
This person either totally wanted to freak me out and make me cry (some of my clients really seem to enjoy doing that, actually) or he did not realize that he had used the wrong phrasal verb. He should have said 'looking after', not 'looking for'.

REMEDY:
A *phrasal verb* is basically a *verb (werkwoord)* plus a *preposition (voorzetsel)*, which creates a meaning different from the original verb. We all know what 'to look at' means, right? However, if we add a different preposition at the end of 'to look' (change *at* to another preposition), we actually create a new meaning. If you use the wrong preposition, as my kind fellow above did, then you will cause confusion among your listeners. And maybe a heart attack or two. As I said before, bad grammar can kill.

Let's see what different phrasal verbs can be created with 'to look':

to look after – to take care of —'She had to look after her hamster for three weeks after he got ill from eating that moldy piece of cheese.'

to look at – to see something — 'He couldn't stop looking at his shiny new fake Rolex, because he couldn't believe it only cost five dollars.'

to look away – to not look at something anymore — 'She had to look away when she realized her boyfriend was talking with his mouth full of spinach.'

to look for – to search for something — 'He will never stop looking for the meaning of life.'

to look into – to find out more about something — 'I'm going to look into the idea of starting an underwater ballet school.'

to look out – to watch out for something or to be careful — 'Look out! A UFO is going to land on your head!'

to look through – to examine something quickly — 'I really didn't look through the contract carefully, and ended up buying a pink Cadillac.'

to look up to – to admire someone — 'My sister looks up to people who work hard and help others. I look up to people who are taller than me.'

Extra vitamins!

There are other phrasal verbs you should know. Here are some of the ones we use the most:

TO TAKE:
to take off – to depart or to remove — 'The plane departed at 9.35.' 'She took off her burlap bra because it was itchy.'

to take on – to hire — 'His goldfish therapy institute was growing so fast he had to take on 65 new people last month!'

to take up – to start a new hobby or to fill space or time — 'He took up yoga recently to help him with his back problems.' 'This awesome new book won't take up much space on my shelf.'

to take after – to have a similar appearance or personality — 'She really takes after her mother. I saw them both running to the shoe store when there was a sale!'

to take something back – to return something or to admit you were wrong

— *'He took back the girdle he bought because it was the wrong color.'* *'I'm sorry I said you were ugly. I take it back. You do smell funny, though.'*
to take somebody out – to go out with someone and pay for them — *'He finally got over his nerves and took her out to an all-you-can-eat steakhouse. He then found out she was a vegetarian.'*

TO GET:
to get around – to have mobility — *'He was forced to get around in a wheelchair after his failed attempt at banana-peel ballet.'*
to get over something or someone – to recover from someone or something — *'She will never get over him, as he was the first one to tell her that her braces were sexy.'*
to get back at someone – to get revenge — *'They decided to get back at the rival gang by beating them at the next round of Gangsta Chess.'*
to get back into something – to become interested in something again — *'I got back into my Circus Clown Training program the minute I heard that it was subsidized!'*
to get away with something – to do something without being noticed or punished — *'He always gets away with cheating on his spelling tests! That's not fair!'*
to get up – to get out of bed in the morning — *'I always get up when I set four alarm clocks!'*

There is a big difference between 'getting up' and 'waking up'.
You can get up long before you wake up. I get up at 6.30 but I finally wake up around 9 A.M.!

(Oh, and if you 'stand up' in the morning, this means that you were sitting all morning, like in a courtroom, for example, and then you stood up when the judge walked in.)

DON'T GO THERE

And now, my love, I end with my final 'Don't Go There' list. Promise me you'll never say these again.

'To my opinion, this could really be a problem.'
Oy. Talk about problems! This should be 'in my opinion', which brings me to the following:

'I have no meaning.'
Actually, darling, you do. You do have a meaning. We all have a special meaning or purpose in life. Yours just isn't to speak excellent English. You may not have an opinion about something, though. Do you know what I mean?

'I have no ID.'
I am not asking for your passport. Or your birth certificate. Or even your driver's license. What I would like to know, however, is your idea. Just pretend the word 'idea' ends with a 'ja!' sound. This way you will think people are enthusiastic about what you have to say.

'I am married with her since two years.'
Oh, that's just wonderful – congratulations! I can only assume that your wife is not a grammar teacher, because she might have left you by now. You are married *to* someone, and if you use a period of time (days/weeks/months/years, etc), then you need to use *for* and not *since*. We use *since* to talk about when (the day, date, or time) the action started: 'since Monday', 'since I woke up this morning', or 'since I bought this awesome book'.

'The doctor gave me a recipe.'
The first time I heard this I freaked out – I thought you had to make your own medicine in Holland! You can get a prescription for medicine, a subscription to a magazine, a club membership, or a recipe to make awesome fudge brownies. If you have one, let me know!

'He wore a smoking to his wedding.'
A smoking what? It sounds like a very dangerous outfit. Did his bride run away? If he wore a tuxedo or a smoking jacket (just to let you know, Hugh Hefner, the founder of *Playboy*, is known for his vast collection of smoking jackets), a dinner jacket, or if he went in black tie...all of these sound like a much safer fashion option.

'You look good on that picture.'
Thank you, that's very kind of you to say so, but if you really want to compliment me, say I look good *in* the picture. You look good in the mirror, in the film, in the photograph. And you do!

'I made a lot of good photos on vacation.'
Did you actually make them yourself? In a darkroom? Otherwise, you just *take* a photograph. And then you post it on Facebook, of course!

'Hardly welcome on our show.'
I bet someone really felt hardly welcome after hearing this! It's 'Welcome to our show.'

'Or you do this or you do that – it's up to you.'
Well, if it were up to me, you never would have said this sentence. You're confusing the Dutch 'of...of' construction with 'either...or' in English. Don't do that. Thank you!

Darling! Honey pie! Sugar plum...you DID IT! You've gone through the first part of the book and have lived to tell about it! I'm so very proud of you – I knew you could do it! Thank you so much for sticking with me on the Buffi Rollercoaster. I so loved having you as a copilot (except that time when you sneezed in this book and got it all sticky).

I CAN'T WAIT TO SEE YOU SOON IN *Section Two!* →

Section Two

SECTION TWO

LET'S GET DOWN TO BUSINESS, YO

The second part of this book was created to make you feel like a rock star at work. I want you to speak English with confidence and flair, whether it's during an informal network chat or negotiating an international deal. I have organized this section into different subsections. Each one deals with a particular aspect of professional communication in English.

I hope it will put some swagger in your step, a smile on your gorgeous face, and get you some high fives (and/or fist bumps) from your (very impressed) colleagues.

Ready? Sure you are.

CHAPTER 4

PRESENTATIONS
Let's Put The 'Present' Back In 'Presentation'

Presentations actually happen more often than people think. It's not just standing in front of a group with a projector and a pie chart (with some homemade, gluten-free chocolate pie on the table, which, by the way, I highly recommend) – it could be explaining corporate policy to your new colleague over coffee, or showing a prospective client around your building, for example. I hope these tips and tricks will help you nail these kinds of talks, too.

31. HOW TO TRIPLE YOUR VOCABULARY FAST (AND MAKE THE RIGHT CONNECTION)

I think that when you talk to someone you should make them feel warm and kind of special inside. You can do this in different ways. You can give them a huge shot of vodka, or you can communicate in a way that makes them feel connected to you. I always say start with the second way, and if that doesn't work, then try the vodka. Talking to people creates a bond. You need to have enough vocabulary to express yourself well to make that connection in English. However, many people don't have enough tools to do this. Let me give you my secret formula on how to TRIPLE your vocabulary fast. Lean in, darling (unless you didn't shower today; then just stay right where you are). If you learn a new word, write it down somewhere. In your phone, in an old skool address book (which can easily become your very own personal dictionary — the tabs with letters are already there for you), or any way that works for you. When you look up a new English word (using **www.dictionary.com** or another English–English dictionary, because I don't want you to translate back to your original language when looking up an English word, like, EVER), find a word that means the same. This is called a *synonym* (**www.thesaurus.com** is also a great resource for this). Then find an *antonym* (this is a word that means the opposite). Your new word is A. Your synonym is B.

Your antonym is C. And my Magic Formula For Tripling Your Vocabulary Fast is... (drum roll, please)....

$$A = B \neq C$$

That's it. A equals B but does not equal C. You learn three words for the effort of one. For example: A = *good*, B = *pleasant* and C = *bad*. This approach is actually easier, because you now have other words to link your new word to. Your brain can remember this little cluster (or Terrific Trilogy, if you are so inclined) as a unit, instead of just trying to remember random words. Picture them linked together in your mind. And write a sentence for each one. Activate them as much as you can, and if you've used A in a sentence, try to use B the next time, so that you're not using the same word over and over again. It's that simple. And it works. Once your vocabulary grows, you will have more ways to reach out to people, as your language will become richer and more complex, and you won't struggle as much to find the right word. Try it. Today!

32. KILL THOSE NERVES AND B-R-E-A-T-H-E

So many people get nervous before they have to talk to people, especially when it's in front of a group. I totally get this. This happens to me when I have to give an interview in Dutch on live TV or radio. However, I have found a technique that really works well. And fast. It's free, and you can do it any time (although I wouldn't recommend doing it while operating heavy machinery, driving, or performing surgery). Let me talk you through it here. Sit comfortably, uncross your legs, and close your eyes. (Oh, wait, first READ THIS and then close your eyes.) You're going to breathe in through your nose for a count of 4 (each 'count' is about a second). Then you're going to hold that breath for a count of 7. Then you're going to exhale, making the F sound, slow and low, for a count of 8. Then you inhale again through your nose for a count of 4 and repeat this cycle. In for 4, hold for 7, exhale slow and low for 8. I usually do this for about 5 rounds and most clients really feel a difference when they (slowly) open their eyes. There is less tension in their necks and their shoulders are lower and more relaxed. Many people have told me that they feel clearer, more balanced, and more focused afterwards. Try it for yourself the next time you have a stressful situation. I'm curious about what it will bring you!

33. KNOW YOUR AUDIENCE (AND GET SUSHI)

Most people think that giving a presentation is all about them. Actually it's not. It's about your audience. You need to think about them first. And then you prepare. If you prepare your talk without knowing who you are talking to, you might be setting yourself up for failure. And that sucks. Try to find out who you are talking to first. How big is the group? What do they already know about the subject? What do they already know about me? How can I find the right 'hook' to get them into the heart of my story?

Let's say that I love fishing (let's first say that that is a lie, but still...). Let's then say I take all my hard-earned pennies and I use them to buy the fattest worms I can find. I go out with my bucket (or box? Or bag? I am not up to date on how worms are packaged these days) and wait for the fish to bite. And guess what? Nothing. Bupkes. Nada. Why? It turns out that the fish I'm trying to catch only eat bread. And alas, this means no sushi for me, as I ended up empty-handed (or empty-hooked). I didn't make an effort to find out what they'd be interested in first, before I got out there and started. So put your audience first. And then pass the wasabi.

34. KNOW YOUR PURPOSE

After you have determined WHO you are talking to, then it's time to focus on WHY. Why are you there? Are you there to educate? Are you there to convince them of something? Are you there to defend a controversial concept? Are you pitching a new idea? If you really think hard about WHY you are there, then you can start shaping your message. Different strokes for different folks. If you forget this important step in your preparation, then you will fall back on your old habits and talk about your subject in the way you have always done before – without considering the real essence of why you are there. And that might not work for this particular group. Put them first, put the purpose second, and then sit down and start prepping. Which leads me to my next point...

35. KNOW YOUR SHIZZLE

Of course you have to know what you are talking about. There must be a reason why you were asked to talk in the first place, right? So. Let's talk about your talk. It's so important that you know your material back and forth. Practice. Practice while you're stuck in traffic, practice while you're washing the dishes (or bribing your kids to do them), practice while you're running (in the park or to the train) in the morning. Make sure you know your story inside and out. A very helpful tip is to record your talk and then listen to yourself. Did you repeat a word too many times? Did you say 'uh...' or 'you know...' too much? Were there too many gaps in your talk? Present for other people and get their honest feedback. This means presenting to people who are objective. Who may not love every single thing you do. Who can sit still, listen critically, and give you constructive feedback on what they saw and heard. The more honest feedback you get, the more you can apply it and learn from it. And the more you (and your audience) will benefit from it!

36. INTRODUCTION TO AWESOMENESS

When giving a presentation, it's important to put your audience at ease right away. That's a big part of your job and something that gets overlooked far too often, unfortunately. It's your responsibility to make your audience feel comfortable, and to get them excited about hearing your story. If someone in the audience doesn't know how long you'll be talking for, or has no idea when (or even IF) they can ask questions, they will not feel relaxed. They might be distracted while you are talking. They might be thinking *'Um, can I ask something? Should I wait? Does anyone else look confused? Should I raise my hand...? Is now a good time...?'* If this is what is happening in their heads, they are slipping away from you and focusing on their own internal situation. And once your audience starts to slip away, it's hard to get them back. If you cover some basic points in the first minute or two of your introduction, you've got your bases covered and are ready to rock. Some things to think about are: 1. Who am I? 2. Why am I here? 3. How long will it take? 4. When can you take questions? Let me give you an example where all the bases are covered:

'Hi, my name is Shirley. Thank you for coming today. I'm so happy to be here! I'm going to share my story about how I became a celebrity poodle groomer, and my talk should take about 15 minutes. There will be time at the end for all of your questions. Now let's get started.'

This was a great introduction – all the bases were covered, and it took about 15 seconds to say (yes, I practiced). Let's look back on that intro. Shirley introduced herself and acknowledged the audience by thanking them for coming. Always start with a word of thanks to make your audience feel welcome and appreciated. I call this the First Magic Thank You Moment. Who doesn't love a pat on the back from time to time (maybe someone with a recent stab wound, but that's another story)? She then stated simply what her talk was about and how long it would take. This makes people feel more comfortable, as they know when they can go to the bathroom, check their emails, see another meme of a cat playing the piano, and check Instagram to see how many likes their latte got that morning. They also know when they can ask questions. I usually train people to get through their story first and then deal with audience questions at the end. Of course, you can say 'Feel free to interrupt me at any time if you have any questions,' if you are so inclined. However, the danger in doing this is that someone might have a question based on the answer you just gave someone else, and it is easy to spiral away from your original talk. If you feel super-confident, and have the time to do this, then of course let your audience know that they can ask you questions at any time. However, if you want to play it safe, get through your material first before you get to Question Time.

Of course, if your audience has a timetable or program where it's stated clearly who you are and what you are talking about, and if the length of your talk is also known, then you can adapt your intro accordingly. However, don't forget to thank your audience for coming. We love being thanked. Sprinkle gratitude around like stardust. It works!

37. THE WOW FACTOR

Sometimes you just want to start your presentation with a Huge Slice Of Awesomeness In Their Face. A great way to do this is to start with The Wow Factor

– getting the audience in from the get-go with an emotional trigger or question. This is used all the time in TED talks, and I often train people to do this when I'm working on their TEDx talk. If appropriate, you can bypass the 'standard' intro that I described above and just cut to the chase with a statement or question that works on an emotional level and brings your audience in right away. Something like, 'Imagine a world where all children are fed...' or 'I have 192 things on my bucket list, and one of them is this talk...' or 'Let's say you have a million dollars to share with the world – what would you do first...?' Or, in Shirley's case above, she might want to say something like 'Imagine a world where all poodles are perfect. I create that world every day.'

This gets people thinking (and feeling!) right away and is an effective method to cut through to the heart of your story right at the start. Try it and see how people react!

38. A TOTALLY TERRIFIC TEMPLATE

Part of knowing how to prepare is thinking hard about what you want to say. And then thinking about how you want to say it. It's important to create a clear structure in order to get your message across well. I have found a simple, yet very effective template which will help you structure your next presentation. Here it is.

1. Introduction And First Magic Thank You Moment
2. Body of Talk (With Subtopics And Connecting Language)
3. Summary
4. Conclusion
5. Second Magic Thank You Moment
6. Question Time
7. Final Thank You Moment And Leave Them (Wanting More)

Let's go through this together:

Intro: We have already discussed this in the previous points. If you don't remember, flip back, scroll back, or take a nap because you must be really tired. And don't forget to thank the audience for showing up! (That's the First Magic Thank You Moment.)

Body of Talk: Think of what you want to say and the order in which you want to say it. Then use connecting phrases to link each point to the next one. The next page will go more into detail on helpful phrases you can use for connecting your ideas to make your presentation 'flow' better.

Summary: This is basically a roundup of the most important points you have just covered. If someone has fallen asleep during your presentation, and they wake up in time for the summary, they will still get the main ideas that you were trying to share in your talk. And they should be filled with guilt for not staying awake!

Conclusion: This is your final statement before going into Question Time. The next page will give you some handy phrases for sharing your conclusion.

Second Magic Thank You Moment: This is your time to thank your audience once again and then open the floor to questions. (I know you already thanked them in the beginning for showing up, but it's always a good idea to thank them for listening. Except for the guy who fell asleep. Forget about him.)

Question Time: On page 108 we will go more into detail about how to handle Question Time with helpful phrases and tips on how to deal with questions you have no answer for.

Final Thank You Moment And Leave Them (Wanting More): Thank everyone for coming, tell them how much you enjoyed talking to them, and give them the idea that you can still come back for more as you still have lots more fabulousness to share with them! It's also important that they know how to contact you in the future. Sometimes this is written on the program, however. Just check (as part of your preparation) how much they know about you already and if they know how to reach you for a possible follow-up talk in the future. Then it's gin o'clock, as you are officially done (once you have asked your audience to sit down, as I am sure you will have gotten a standing ovation by now).

39. LET'S GET CONNECTED!

An important part of dealing with information and facts when it comes to presentations is making the way you talk about them 'flow'. You want your information to be interesting and pleasant to hear, not boring or dry. Your presentation should sound connected, not like a list of bullet points. A good way to work on creating that flow when you talk is to focus on connecting words and phrases.

Here are some ways to do that:
- 'I've divided my talk into three parts. First I'll be telling you about...then I'll have a look at...and the last part of my presentation will be on...'

- 'That wraps up the first part of my talk. Now I'd like to turn our attention to the next part, which focuses on....'

- 'If we have a look at this chart, you'll see what I'm referring to in the next part of my talk today...'

- '...and that leads me to the following point, which is about...'

- 'Right, that ends the second part of my talk...'

- 'That's all I'd like to say about...for now.'

- 'I'd like to end by emphasizing the main points I've covered today...'

- 'I'd like to wind it up by saying...'

- 'Before I open the floor to questions, I'd just like to summarize my main points...'

If you work on having a good start and ending to each point you're trying to make by actually 'packaging' your message in between these two phrases, it will have a huge impact on the 'flow' and the 'feel' of your presentation. Connecting your ideas leads to a better connection with your audience!

40. DEALING WITH QUESTIONS

As I stated before, there are two different options for dealing with questions. One of them is to be interrupted at any time, and the other is to hold the questions until the end of your talk. Here are some helpful phrases you can use for these situations:

• *'Please feel free to interrupt me at any time during my talk if you have a question.'*

• *'Should you have a question, don't hesitate to ask me during my presentation.'*

• *'I'm happy to hear your questions whenever you have them, so just shout out if you've got one!'*

• *'I'd appreciate it if you held your questions until the end of my talk.'*

• *'There will be plenty of time at the end of my talk for answering any questions you might have. Thank you for your patience!'*

• *'I'd love to hear all your questions, but in the interest of time it's best if we wait until the end of my talk. Thanks!'*

And...what do you do if you get a question you don't know the answer to? You answer honestly. Don't lie because that shit will be on YouTube by the end of the day and you'll seem like a fraud. Just say honestly that you don't know the answer. This could be a great opportunity to open it up to the audience and get them involved – feel free to ask them if anyone else has the answer. Be careful about saying 'I don't know, but I'll look it up and get back to you.' This could be effective, but I tried it and it didn't work for me. I said that exact phrase in my response a few years ago, when I got a question I didn't know the answer to, and the next day I got dozens of emails from other people in the audience asking me questions about other things (mostly not related to my presentation) as well. I guess they thought 'Well, since she's mailing him personally about that, maybe she can answer my question too?' It wasn't my intention to hear from so many people about what was on their minds at the time. I've changed my approach — now I say 'I don't know the answer, but I will look it up and put your question and my answer in my newsletter next week, so that everyone can benefit!' Winky smiley face. But it works!

41. IT'S ALL ABOUT THE NIPPLES
(Yes, I Said 'Nipples')

Many people feel more comfortable using notes when they have to speak in public. That's fine. What's not fine is how most people use them during their talk. I know the upper-forehead region of many people better than I would like to know. This is because they leave their notes on the table and bend down to read them while they are talking. This is a big no-no, no matter how gorgeous your forehead is. Don't go there, darlings. Take your notes up to you. But never raise them above your nipples. If you look closely at the news readers and journalists on TV, you will notice that their notes are never raised above their nipples. Their heads keep on talking and maintaining contact with us, as they are never blocked or obstructed by paper (or a tablet). Just pretend you are a talking head on TV when you speak (and doing a little dance to the Talking Heads might also be a great way to warm up for your talk, but that's another story).

Oh, and about your notes – please keep in mind that the more you write down, the easier it is to get lost in your notes. Try to keep it simple and clear – just a few key words or phrases to get you through your presentation might just be enough. If you use note cards, make sure you number them. Why? Because if you get nervous and drop them on the floor, it's so embarrassing watching you put them back in a panic in the right order. Let me save your ass right now and tell you to number your cards. Believe me. You don't want to see what happens if you don't!

42. THE THIRD EYE

I coach a lot of music artists. Rock stars, pop idols, singer/songwriters, heavy metal gods...you name it, I've worked with them. And I love it! Many times I go to their shows (yeah, it's a tough job, but someone's got to do it). Once I was in the back of the club (sippin' on the bub), watching my clients rock the house. Standing in front of me was a group of 17-year-old girls. They sighed and swooned when the lead singer was doing his thang. At one point, during a sensitive ballad, one of them said 'Did you see that? He was looking right at me! Our eyes locked! OMG!' Maybe she even thought that the song he was singing was about her – that's just how connected she felt to the singer. He looked directly at her, and she felt it.

The funny thing is, I know he couldn't see her. At all. He was blinded by the spotlights, as most artists are when they are on stage.

How do you create an eye-lock with your audience, even if you cannot see them? There are different ways to do this. You can 'scan' the audience with your eyes. Take a moment to acknowledge every person in the room. Many people remember more when they feel acknowledged and included. Creating eye contact is an excellent way to do that. However, many people feel uncomfortable, especially in a smaller, more intimate group, if they have to look someone right in the eye. This I understand. When I lived in New York, it was an unwritten rule that you didn't have eye contact on the subway or in other public places. This was considered too direct, and in some cases, could be interpreted to be threatening. So I developed a coping mechanism that I still use to this day. I look people in their third eye.

Say what?!?!

The third eye is the place just between your eyebrows, right above where your nose starts. (If you have a unibrow, get that waxed first.) If you look at someone's third eye, they will never know that you are not looking them right in the eye. Try it – you'll be surprised how effective it is!

CHAPTER 5

NEGOTIATIONS
Getting The 'Go' Back in Negotiations
(And Meetings, Although There's No 'Go' In That Word)

I am fortunate to be the personal English coach to some very talented and passionate corporate executives. One of the things they struggle with the most is getting their message across effectively and professionally during meetings and negotiation sessions. I hope this section helps you walk into your next session feeling like a million bucks. (Or euros.)

43. A WARM WELCOME

Once I went to a first-time meeting with a prominent CEO. He greeted me with 'Hi. Sit down.' I did what he said, but I felt like he was going to ask me to roll over and beg in a minute. As I said earlier in the presentation section, an important part of having good communication skills is making people feel welcome and appreciated. You never get a second chance to make a first impression. Now, I'm not asking for a back rub or a gin and tonic the minute I walk into a room, but starting off like he did for the first meeting might come across as being a bit abrupt, aggressive, or blunt. Let's find some other ways to welcome people to a meeting or a negotiation session. How about these?

- *I would like to welcome you to...*
- *On behalf of...I would like to welcome you to...*
- *It's my pleasure to welcome you to...*
- *How was your flight?*
- *Lovely/nice to finally meet you.*
- *Would you like something to drink?*
- *Is this your first visit to...?*
- *Great to see the face behind the name.*

If you start by welcoming someone in this way, it's just a matter of time before a gin and tonic appears! (The back rub is optional.)

44. TERMS AND CONDITIONALS

As discussed on page 78, we use conditionals (a fancy way of naming *if* clauses in sentences) in order to talk about hypothetical situations and the possible consequences of them. I'd like to apply them now to negotiation sessions in English. They're so helpful and they are so often overlooked!

We discussed earlier the difference between *if* and *when*. In case you've forgotten, let me gently remind you. *If* is used for hypothetical situations, and *when* is used for things that are really going to happen; you just don't know when they are going to happen. For example, 'If it rains, I'll cancel our picnic,' but 'When it rains, you get wet.'

See the difference? We use *if* quite a lot when negotiating, to show that we have not yet committed to an agreement or a contract. We have three types of conditionals, and now I'd like to show you how you can apply each one to your next negotiation session.

45. CONDITIONALS TYPE 1: THE PROMISE

The structure is quite straightforward:

If + the present simple > will/can/may + the rest of the sentence.

This type of conditional is used for something that could realistically happen. It's used for making a promise, and you'll hear it used quite frequently at the start of negotiation sessions, when you're trying to get off on the right foot (which, by the way, is a great expression and you should try and use it sometime. Like today. Thanks!).

Here are some handy phrases you could think of using:
'If you lower your prices, we will consider increasing our order.'
'If you deliver a month earlier, we can make our deadline.'
'If she approves the budget, we may hire two new staff members next year.'

You can also flip the word order around, and put the *if* in the middle of the sentence. This kind of word-order flip is something that doesn't happen very much in English, so I hope you appreciate this very special moment in your learning life:
'We will consider increasing our order if you lower your prices.'
'We can make our deadline if you approve the budget.'
'We may hire two new staff members next year if she approves the budget.'

Now take a few minutes to complete the following sentences.
'If you are interested in our services, we will...'
'If our new policy is passed, we can...'
'We may change offices if....'
'He will contact you if...'

46. CONDITIONALS TYPE 2: WHEN DOUBT ENTERS THE ROOM

These are used in a different way than Type 1. We use them to talk about situations we are not totally sure of. It's not making a promise, it's actually expressing doubt or skepticism about something. This is a subtle but effective approach when it comes to negotiations!

Let's compare Type 1 and Type 2 so that you can see the difference. Let's say that you have a friend who weighs 600 kilos and is in poor health. He went to the doctor and the doctor said, 'If you go to the gym, you will feel better.' A month later he is still complaining about not feeling well, and he hasn't gone to the gym. You could then say to him, 'If you went to the gym, you'd feel better!' This is your way of telling him to get his ass in the gym. Subtle, yet effective!

The structure of these conditionals is slightly different than Type 1. We use the past simple for these. The magic formula is:

If + past simple > would/could/might + rest of the sentence.

Let's see how the feeling of the sentences above changes when we put them into a Type 2 conditional structure:
'If you lowered your prices, we would consider increasing our order.'
'If you delivered a month earlier, we could make our deadline.'
'If she approved the budget, we might hire two new staff members next year.'

Do you see how the mood has changed? It sounds like you are more doubtful, skeptical, or putting more pressure on your counterpart. This can be an effective technique to use when appropriate.

This form is also used for speculation – trying to imagine what would happen *if...* Let's try to complete some of these structures in your own way. Can you complete the following questions? (Yes, you can.)
'If my boss gave me a raise, I could...'
'If you could change one thing about your work, it would be...'
'If I lost my job, I would...'
'I could learn how to...if I only had more...'

47. LOOKING BACK

We use Type 3 conditionals in a different way to Types 1 and 2. Type 1 looks ahead, to a realistic situation; Type 2 looks ahead with doubt, skepticism, or something that's not realistic in its expectations, but Type 3, my friend (I feel that close to you now after sharing so many pages together), is different. It's used to talk about a situation that has already happened. It's looking back, often with a feeling of regret or nostalgia. It's an excellent way to bring bad news, or explain why a situation went the way it did (for better or for worse). The structure is a bit trickier than the others, and goes like this:

If + past perfect > would have/could have/ might have + past participle + rest of sentence.

Wow, that's quite a formula. Let's see it in action in a negotiation session:
'If you had lowered our prices, we would have increased our order.' (But you didn't, so we didn't. Your loss!)
'If you had delivered a month earlier, we could have made our deadline.' (But we didn't make our deadline because you didn't deliver earlier, so now we are really pissed off.)
'If she had approved our budget, we might have hired more people.' (This is what you say to your awful neighbor who is looking for a job at your company.)

Type 3 is also a great way to get out of a tricky situation. For example:
'If you had told me you needed this report done by Friday, I would have finished it by then!' (But you didn't tell me, you stupid moron, and that's why I thought I had a month to do it. Not. My. Fault.)
'If we had only bought those shares when they were a dollar each, we would have had a million dollars by now!' (And we are living on instant noodles because we didn't buy those damn shares in time. Kind of sucks.)

I hope now you have a better understanding on how to apply these three conditionals to your next negotiation session! Keep this book under the table in case you need some extra help!

48. DON'T MAKE AN ASS OUT OF U AND ME

An important part of negotiations (and meetings, of course!) is to check for agreement as you go along. Never assume that the other party agrees with you completely, or that they even understand everything that you are discussing. (Did you know we have an expression in English about this? It's 'Never *assume*, because when you assume you make an **ass** out of **u** and **me**!' OK, you can stop laughing hysterically now. Just enjoy this new Golden Nugget of Knowledge.) Here are some handy phrases to check for agreement as you continue your negotiations:
'It seems that...'
'Are you suggesting that...'
'Do you mean...'
'If I understood you correctly...'
'What exactly do you mean by...?'

'I'm not sure I fully understand your point.'
'Could you clarify one point for me?'
'Would you like to elaborate on that?'
'Could you be more specific?'
'In other words, you feel that...'
'Can we summarize your position up to this point?'

Note: Most of these phrases also work when discussing curfew with teenagers. Just sayin'.

49. MY RECIPE FOR A BAD NEWS SANDWICH

Many times people struggle when it comes to giving bad news. I understand completely. Giving bad news is hard enough, but if you can 'soften' the way you say it, it really makes a difference in how people perceive your message. It's best to start with something positive, then say the bad news, and then end with something positive. Here's an example:

'Thank you for clarifying your position. Unfortunately, we are unable to agree at this point, but we'd like to meet again next quarter to discuss further options.'

This is a very pleasant way of expressing disagreement. This person (well, me, actually) started with a positive statement by thanking the person, then got to the point of the message – that I disagreed – but then ended it with a hopeful follow-up meeting suggestion.

Here's another one:
'It's clear that you're enthusiastic about joining our company. We really appreciate that. However, we are looking for someone with more experience in the work field at this time. Do contact us in the future if this becomes the case!'

So instead of saying 'You're not the right person for the job,' you've said the same message but in a lovely sandwich. This means that the person leaving your office will leave less depressed, and might feel inspired to try again in the future.

Now you might be saying, 'Oh, this sounds so American. Why can't we just say the bad news and leave it at that?' I hear this all the time. And yes, of course you can just give it to them straight. Sometimes this could actually be the best strategy. However, when it comes to being (and staying) polite in professional situations, a bit of delicate wording can make all the difference. I honestly feel, at the end of the day, people may not remember what you did for them, but they remember how you made them feel. If you can make someone feel respected, despite having to give them bad news, then why not try doing so?

Who knows? A Bad News Sandwich might just end up being your favorite recipe for the office. Bring one to your next 'We are over budget' party.

50. A COMPROMISING SITUATION

When having a meeting or a negotiation session in English, it's important to figure out how flexible you can be or want to be, and in what areas. If you don't figure this out ahead of time, it could lead to confusion when you have to get down to the nitty gritty. Here are some useful phrases to help you examine and create a compromise with your counterpart.

'How flexible can you be on that?'
'In return for this, would you be willing to...?'
'May we offer an alternative?'
'We are ready to accept your offer; however, there would be one condition.'
'We feel there has to be/needs to be a trade-off here.'
'We would be willing to..., provided, of course, that...'
'We'd be prepared to... However, there's just one condition.'

Try using some of these phrases in your next meeting or negotiation session and see what happens! Oh, and by the way, if you successfully negotiate a trillion-dollar deal because all of a sudden your English got a lot better because of...well...using this book, do remember the person who wrote it, OK? Wink wink. Nudge nudge. Thank you!

CHAPTER 6

AGREEING AND DISAGREEING
And Asking What They Think

People tend to forget that agreeing and disagreeing can be raised to an art form. I hear far too often the same words or phrases when it comes to business conversations. You can do better, darling. Establishing agreement, or expressing disagreement clearly (but politely!) is essential when it comes to professional communication. And having the right phrases at hand to ask someone's opinion in just the right way might very well be your secret weapon to winning them over at your next meeting.

AGREEING: SAY YES (NOT JUST TO THE DRESS)

If you're always agreeing in the same way, there's a good chance that it might not always be appropriate or professional. You can do a lot more than just saying OK. A big part of this book is to get you out of your comfort zone and try new ways of expressing yourself. In this section, I'd like to show you different ways to express not only complete agreement but also partial agreement in English, as many people find this tricky.

51. HELL, YEAH
(How To Agree Completely, Totally, And Wholeheartedly)

So, you want to show them the love? Here are some useful phrases to use when you feel like nodding your head emphatically, as you are in total and utter agreement:
'I totally agree with you.'
'I fully/completely agree.'
'I'm in total agreement.'
'Absolutely!'
'I know!'
'I totally get that.'

54. SO CLOSE...AND YET SO FAR
(Expressing Partial Disagreement)

If you disagree with someone (or something), it's very helpful if you leave the door of communication (yes, that's a thing) open, even if it's just a crack. If you only say 'That doesn't work for me' and you don't say WHY, you are slamming that door shut. And no one likes a door slammed in their face, right? Right. So leave it open by being clear about what you need to see happen in order to reach agreement. Here are some phrases that might help you achieve this:

'That's not exactly how I saw it. If you could consider...'
'We actually had something else in mind. How about...'
'From our point of view, this needs to happen...'
'If you can go along with us on this point, then we have a deal!'
'I don't see a problem with...but I'd like to see...as well.'
'That might work, depending on....'
'We were hoping to get to...today.'
'If you consider our position, you'll see that we need...'

55. HIT ME BABY ONE MORE TIME
(Using Time Indications To Leave The Door Open)

A very effective way of saying no without closing the communication door (God, I love that image) completely is to use time indicators. These are words that tell your counterpart that maybe something might not work right now, but it doesn't mean your disagreement is written in stone. Giving someone the idea that your disagreement might be temporary could create a very hopeful situation indeed! Here are some helpful phrases for that:

'I'm afraid we are unable to commit at this time.'
'At present, it seems like this is not where we need to go.'
'I'm afraid it's a no for now.'
'Our team cannot agree to that at the present time.'
'Unfortunately, the present circumstances are not favorable.'
'Right now it looks like it's a no go.'
'Looks like this is where we'll have to stay for this quarter.'

IT'S NOT ALL ABOUT YOU: ASKING OTHERS WHAT THEY THINK

OK, darling, I think we've talked enough for now about you. Let's find out what other people think. There are several ways to ask other people about their opinion. If you've always said 'What do you think?', you are missing out. Try some of these phrases on for size! I have divided them into formal and informal styles.

56. R-E-S-P-E-C-T
(Find Out What It Means To Them)

Here are some different ways to ask someone about his or her opinion, in a formal style. These phrases will prove to be quite useful if you ever need to call the queen or President Obama for advice. You never know. I want you to be prepared for everything!

'I'm very curious as to your opinion on this matter.'
'I'm very interested to hear your views on this.'
'What's your perspective on this?'
'What are your views on this?'
'I'd like to know your point of view on this situation.'
'Could you tell me how you feel about this?'
'Would you mind telling me your opinion regarding this?'

57. TELL ME WHAT YOU WANT
(What You Really, Really Want)

There are many informal ways to ask someone's opinion. These are great to use for your close colleagues, your drinking buddies, and other familiar creatures. Let's see if any of these work for you:
'Can you let me know what you think about this?'
'Where do you stand?'
'What do you think about this?'
'What's your take/angle on this?'
'What do you reckon?'

'How do you feel about it?'
'Please tell us your opinion.'
'I'm dying to know what you think!'
'I'd love to hear what you think about this.'

So, my dear, what do you think? Where do you stand when it comes to asking people about their opinion? I'm dying to know how you feel about this! (See what I did there?)

CHAPTER 7

TELEPHONE SKILLS
'I Know When That Hotline Blings, It Can Only Mean One Thing'

I know that you know how to use the phone, but are you getting enough out of your phone conversations? I wanted to devote a few pages to this phenomenon. If you are always using the same vocabulary when it comes to phone skills, there's a good chance that the people you are interacting with are bored. And you just might be too! So let's get busy!

MAKING A PHONE CALL

58. 'HELLO, IT'S ME': INTRODUCING YOURSELF

There are different ways to introduce yourself, depending on how well you know the person. If you'd like to take a formal approach, for someone you don't know or someone who is 'higher up' in the professional chain, here are some options:
- *'Good morning, this is Lisa Johnson from Ikea calling.'* (Of course, if you don't work for Ikea, don't say this, unless it's April 1.)
- *'Hello, this is Ben Sandman ringing from ABC Incorporated.'* (Side note: 'Ringing' is used more in the UK, and 'calling' is used more in the US.)

However, if you already know the person you are calling, you can easily take it down a notch and get short and sweet:
'Hey, it's George!'
'Hi, Susan here.'
'Morning, it's me, Lillian.'

59. 'WHO YOU GONNA CALL?': ASKING FOR SOMEONE

There are different ways to go about doing this. Here are some formal and informal phrases that will give you more variety when it comes to asking for someone. Or just calling Ghostbusters, if you are so inclined.

FORMAL:
'May I speak to Ms Jackson, please?'
'Could I talk to Sally, please?'
'Is George in today, by any chance?'
'I was wondering if I could talk to Mr Hanson.'
'I'm trying to reach Bridget. Could you put me through, please?'
'I'd like to talk to Janet, please.'
'Could I talk to someone from Marketing, please? Thanks!'

INFORMAL:
'Hey, is Phil around?'
'Hi, is Dan in?'
'Morning, is Betty there?'
'Hey, can you get Annie for me? Thanks!'
'John around?' (Actually, be careful if you use this phrase with the name 'Dick'. Because 'dicking around' means something in English. Don't make me go there. Thank you.)
'Peter, please. Thanks!'

60. ICE, ICE, BABY
(And How To Break It)

It's usually (but not always) a good idea to break the ice with a bit of small talk before you get to the reason why you're calling.

'How did the launch go last week?'
'How are things in Brussels?'
'So, I guess you survived the blizzard/hurricane/alien attack I read about? Glad you're OK!'

'How was your holiday?'
'Did you see/catch that game last night?' (Only ask this if you know they are an avid sports fan and are referring to their favorite club winning.)
'How are your children getting on at school?'
'I saw your update on LinkedIn. Congratulations!'

61. TELL ME WHY (YOU ARE CALLING)

It's always a good idea to state why you are calling. Unless, of course, it's just a 'friendly' call to catch up, which is also an excellent way to network and keep the communication flame a-burning. You don't always have to wait until you have a fire to put out to contact someone!

FORMAL:
'I'm ringing in regard to our recent mail conversation...'
'I'm calling about your price quote...'
'I'm interested in finding out more about...'
'I'd like to know your opinion on...'
'I'm ringing on behalf of...'
'Regarding our meeting next week, I'd like to...'
'Concerning our conference, I'd like to...'
'Would you mind telling me more about...'
'I was wondering if you could tell me...'

INFORMAL:
'I just wanted to ask you about...'
'I needed your take on...'
'I wanted to check on the next shipment...'
'Following up on our mails, I'd like to....'
'My boss made me call you. Just joking!'
'Could you give me a quote on...'
'I need some more information about...'

62. TONIGHT'S THE NIGHT: SETTING UP A MEETING

Of course you have a personal assistant, secretary, or robot who always makes appointments for you. But what happens when she or he is ill? Or the robot falls in love with your dishwasher? Then you are on your own. I don't want you to feel stranded or abandoned. You can make your own appointments using these helpful phrases. I promise you: you CAN do this on your own. You got this, honey.

FORMAL:
'I was wondering if we could meet to discuss this.'
'I'd like to set up a meeting to delve into this.' (Delve. Such. A. Great. Word. If you haven't used it before, you are missing out!)
'Would it be possible to set up a Skype meeting about this?'
'Would next week be convenient for you?'
'I'd like to meet at your earliest convenience.' (By the way, this phrase is also very helpful to use in emails, especially when something is urgent. Try 'Please see to this/take care of this at your earliest convenience.' The sense of urgency is masked by politeness. Isn't that cool?)
'Would the first week in June suit you?'
'I'd like to suggest meeting next month. Would that work for you?'

INFORMAL:
'How about meeting face to face on this?'
'Let's get together soon and discuss this.'
'Are you around next week?'
'Can we Skype on this with the team?'
'Does next Friday work for you?'
'How's your schedule for next week shaping up?'
'What's September like for you? Let's set up a meeting.'

63. SORRY SEEMS TO BE THE HARDEST WORD
(How To Change Or Cancel An Appointment Without Pissing Them Off)

Now that you have learned how to make appointments on your own (good for you!, I'm so proud of you!), now let's learn how to cancel them. On page 116 we learned how to make a Bad News Sandwich. This is also very effective when it comes to changing or cancelling an appointment. Sometimes it's best just to give it to them straight, but usually a more gentle approach using 'softening' language works best. Here are some phrases to help you do just that:

(Oh, and remember. You need to check your 'schedule' or your 'calendar', not your 'agenda'! Thanks!)

FORMAL:
'I'm terribly sorry, but I'm afraid I have to cancel our meeting next week.'
'I'm so sorry, but it looks like my schedule has changed.'
'Would it by any chance be possible to move the meeting up a few days?'
'Unfortunately, it looks like I won't be able to make it on the 17th. Could we try for a week later?'
'I would really appreciate it if we could hold the meeting at our office, as I won't be able to travel that day. Would that be possible?'
'Unfortunately, it seems my deadlines have shifted and this means that next week is no longer an option. Could we perhaps find a new date?'

INFORMAL:
'Sorry, but I'm not going to be able to make it next week. Can we take a rain check?'
'How about coming over to our office instead? Looks like I don't have the wiggle room to travel that day.' (Wiggle room. I know it sounds like a very special place where one would go to wiggle, but it's actually a pretty cool phrase which means 'the ability to make small changes in a plan or a schedule.' How fabulous is that? Go wiggle today!)
'Hey, looks like I won't be able to make it after all. How about rescheduling for next Tuesday?'
'You're going to kill me, but I need to postpone our meeting by a week.' (Please remember that postponing something is not the same as cancelling it. It just means delaying an appointment to a later date.)
'You're never going to believe this, but I have a double booking on Friday. Can we reschedule? I'm so sorry.'
'Can we meet an hour later next Wednesday? I don't think I'll make it on time due to a previous appointment. Would be great if we could!'

SECTION TWO

64. 'NO, YOU HANG UP FIRST!': SAYING GOODBYE

It's always hard to say goodbye. And it's even harder when you don't have enough vocabulary to know how to do it well. Here are some phrases to help you say goodbye. Feel free to use these in break-up texts, but only at your own risk. Thank you.

FORMAL:
'It was lovely talking to you.'
'I look forward to meeting you in person.'
'Thank you so much for your time.'
'Thank you for your help/assistance. I really appreciate it.'
'We are looking forward to receiving your proposal. Thanks again for the information.'
'Thank you! You'll be hearing from me again soon. Have a good day!'

INFORMAL:
'Cheers!'
'Thanks again for the update.'
'Was great to reconnect!'
'Speak to you soon!'
'Take care, and talk soon!'
'Can't wait for our next meeting.'
'Really excited to hear about the next step.'
'Have a great day!'
'Let's keep in touch! Ciao!' (For some reason, this sounds better if you are wearing sunglasses and holding a latte when you say it.)

RECEIVING A PHONE CALL

65. PICK UP LINE
(How to Answer the Phone)

If you are an assistant, a secretary, a colleague, or someone who has to answer for (and sometimes to!) other people, some variety in how you do this is usually pretty welcome. Not just for the people who are calling, but more importantly – for you. You don't want to say the same thing every time, do you? (The correct answer here is 'no'.)

FORMAL:
'Good morning, this is Shelly from the XYZ Company, how may I help you?'
'Thank you for calling Philadelphia Flooring. This is Janet speaking. How can I help you?'
'Hello, this is David speaking. How can I help you today?'
'Good afternoon. Thank you for calling Seneca Airways. This is Patrick speaking. How can I assist you today?'

INFORMAL:
'Hello, John's phone.'
'Hi, this is Marianne.'
'Good morning, Seyna here.'
'Hey, it's Lara.'

66. IS IT ME YOU'RE LOOKING FOR?
(Finding Out More)

There are lots of ways to find out who is calling. Here are some different ways to get the scoop.

FORMAL:
'May I ask who's calling, please?'
'Can I ask whom I'm speaking to, please?'
'Could I ask who's calling, please?'
'And who am I talking to, please?'
'Would you mind saying your name, please?'
'I'm sorry, I didn't quite catch your name.'

INFORMAL:
'Who's calling, please?'
'And who's this then?'
'Sorry, I didn't catch your name.'
'Who's this, please?'

67. YOU'RE BREAKING UP: WHAT TO SAY WHEN YOU HAVE A BAD CONNECTION

Speaking English on the phone can be challenging, and even more so when you can't understand what the other person is saying due to a bad connection. Say these lines before hanging up and trying again!

FORMAL:
'I'm afraid I can't hear you very well. Would you mind repeating that, please?'
'I'm sorry, but the line's breaking up. Could you call us back, please?'
'Could you speak up, please? I'm having trouble hearing you.'
'The line is quite bad. Would you mind ringing us again, please?'

INFORMAL:
'Hey, I can't hear you. Let me call you back!'
'Sorry, you're breaking up. Can you call me back?'
'Let me call you right back, the connection is so bad!'
'Hey, are you underwater? I can't hear you! Can you call me back?'

68. YOU GOT ME HANGING ON THE TELEPHONE: HOW TO TAKE MESSAGES

I once called an executive client and his secretary actually told me 'He's sitting on the toilet right now.' I could not believe it. Um, hello, TMI! (This means 'Too much information'. WAAAAAY too much information in this case!) Here are different ways to take messages or to say that a person is not available (no matter what they are doing). Enjoy!

FORMAL:
'I'm sorry, she's not in at the moment. Would you like to leave a message?'
'I'm afraid he's away from his desk right now. Could I take a message?'
'Unfortunately, she's unavailable at the moment.'
'He's not in the office today. Would you like to leave a message?'

'She's in the studio now. Shall I ask her to call you back?'
'He's out of town this week, but would you like to speak to his assistant?'

INFORMAL:
'Hey, sorry but he's out right now. Should I tell him you called?'
'I can't seem to find him anywhere – he's away from his desk. If you leave a message, I'll make sure he gets it!'
'Looks like she's out grabbing lunch. I'll have her call you back when she gets here, OK?'
'Fred's at a conference until Thursday. Would you like to call back then?'
'She's gone home with the flu. Should I tell her you called?'

CHAPTER 8

LIKE A BOSS
Networking Like A Native

Networking is working. It can be really hard if you don't feel comfortable talking to strangers. It can also be a huge challenge when you don't have enough vocabulary to feel confident doing this. Put both of these situations together, and you get a one-way ticket to Awkwardtown. I don't want you to go there. Being in Awkwardtown sucks. It's a lonely, desolate place filled with silence and shame. So let me help you feel better about networking by saying a few things first:

1. Every friend you have ever had started out as a stranger.
2. Many strangers are friends we haven't met yet.
3. Some strangers are total assholes and the only way to find this out is to get to know them.
4. Some of the best things happen during social talks at conferences – I don't mean just getting drunk together and doing the limbo, but planting the seeds of some pretty cool deals and projects which would not have happened otherwise.

So go for it. These helpful phrases will make (and keep!) Awkwardtown really far away.

69. GOOD OLD TIMES

Sometimes it's easy to start networking by reconnecting with people you already know. Here are some phrases to help you get back in touch with someone:
'Hey, Janet, how have you been?'
'I was just scrolling through my LinkedIn contacts and came across your name. How have you been doing?'
'It's been far too long! What have you been up to?'

'I heard about your new job/promotion/ career change/ transfer/book/ film/ signature fragrance – congratulations!'
'I'd love to hear about what you've been up to lately.'
'How about meeting for a drink sometime?'
'I'd love to invite you to our new office!'
'I can't wait to show you around our new building! Let's set a date!'

70. SAY MY NAME, SAY MY NAME: HOW TO INTRODUCE YOURSELF TO NEW PEOPLE

'Hi, I'm Buffi Duberman.' (Try saying this 10 times fast. It's fun.)
'Good morning, my name is Jack Jones. Nice to meet you!'
'Hi [extending hand], Patty Donson. How are you?'
'Hello, I'm Phil from Philips. How do you do?'
'How ya doin'? Howard's the name.' (Cowboy hat optional.)
'Allow me to introduce myself. The name's Bond. James Bond.' (Seriously, how cool would it be to introduce yourself like that?)

~ Golden Nugget of Knowledge ~

Make sure you know when to use 'How do you do?'

This is only used the very first time you meet someone, and it's used more often in British than in American English. Americans tend to say 'How are you?' when meeting someone for the first time. Once you have met someone you can never say 'How do you do?' again, as this phrase is only used for the first encounter. So, the first time you meet someone, you can say either 'How do you do?' (British style) or 'How are you?' (American style). Every time after that, you can say 'How are you?' or 'How have you been?'

Hope that helps!

71. TELL ME MORE: FINDING OUT MORE ABOUT WHAT SOMEONE DOES (AND WHY!)

'What do you do?' (Remember, this is very different from 'What are you doing?' 'What do you do?' refers to your job or profession, and 'What are you doing?' only talks about what you are doing at the moment. See Nr. 21 to find out more.)
'Where do you work?'
'What are you responsible for?'
'How do you know Mary?'
'What department are you associated with?'
'How is the conference going so far?'
'What do you hope to accomplish today?'
'What have you enjoyed the most here this week?'

72. INTRODUCING SOMEONE ELSE

Don't hesitate to bring people together. Building bridges is an essential part of networking!
'Tom, meet Jerry. Jerry, this is Tom, from our cartoon division.'
'Simon, I'd like you to meet Garfunkel. It's about time you both met – you have so much in common!'
'Oh, I'm so sorry. I don't think you two have met. This is Dan, and he's just joined our department!'
'Allow me to introduce my boss. He's a man of wealth and taste.' (If he's not, don't try this.)
'Sorry, I thought you knew each other already. This is our new receptionist, Samuel. Samuel, this is Susan, and she's the head of Marketing.'

73. WELCOME TO MY WORLD: WHAT TO SAY WHEN YOU FORGOT SOMEONE'S NAME.

You don't have to go to Awkwardtown on this one. My grandmother didn't know anyone's name for over 60 years (I think I inherited that gene) and she still was the life of every party!

'I'd love to introduce you, but I'm afraid I've forgotten your name!'
'I'm so sorry, what was your name again?'
'It's so noisy here, I didn't quite catch your name. Could you repeat it, please?'
'Silly me! I seem to have forgotten your name. Could you tell me again, please?'
'I'm so embarrassed. I totally forgot your name. I must be getting old. I'm lucky that I even remember my own name! Mine is Buffi. What's yours?' (I say this daily.)

74. I'LL TELL YOU ALL ABOUT IT WHEN I SEE YOU AGAIN: HOW TO KEEP IN TOUCH

Saying goodbye is such sweet sorrow. Here are some phrases to make sure it won't be too long before your paths connect again.
'Was so great to see you again. Let's keep in touch!'
'Here's my card in case you need to reach me.'
'I really enjoyed meeting you. Let's meet again soon!'
'I hope to see you at next year's conference.'
'I'm going to add you on LinkedIn.'
'Would be great to meet again to discuss this further. Should we set up a meeting?'
'I'd love to keep in touch. Here's my number!'
'I look forward to seeing you again.'
'Looking forward to the next meeting.'
'Hope to welcome you to our office next time!'
'Feel free to contact me if you need anything. Here's my card.'

I hope now you feel more confident and these phrases will help you turn the corner from 'not working' to 'networking'!

SECTION TWO 137

CHAPTER 9

PASSPORT PROOF
English For (Business) Travel

I want you to have no limits when it comes to communicating in English – literally and figuratively. Many of you have to travel for work. I don't believe in separating business from pleasure, as doing business has to be enjoyable. Hopefully these phrases will help you pilot your awesome English skills into international waters and give you more confidence when you have to travel for an international conference or client. We will cover air travel, renting a car, dealing with hotels and restaurants, and shopping (in case you need to bring back bribes for the ones you love).

75. COME FLY AWAY WITH ME

Jet lag is a bitch. Jet lag when you have to be at the top of your game for an international meeting is even more of a bitch. And jet lag when you have to be at the top of your game for an international meeting and you don't have enough vocabulary to sound professional is…well…a super huge bitch.

Let's assume your robot has run away with your dishwasher, and you are forced to make your own flight reservation. These phrases will make it just a bit easier for you.
'I'd like to book a flight, please.'
'I need to make a reservation, please.'
'I'd like to find out what your best price is.'
'Hi, I'm looking for your best rate on…'
'Could you tell me what your rates are, please?'
'I'd like some information about traveling to Boston between July 21st and July 28th.'
'What's the sales tax on that?'
'I'd like a one-way ticket/flight.'
'I'd like a round trip/return ticket/flight.'
'I'd like an open-ended ticket.'

'What is your best rate/price?'
'Could you tell me what my options are during that period, please?'
'I'd like an aisle/window/middle/emergency exit seat.'
'Is that a direct flight?'
'Is there a layover?'
'How long will I have to wait there before changing planes?'
'What are your baggage/luggage limits?'
'How much is the fine for having extra baggage/luggage?'
'What is the weight limit for carry-on luggage?'
'Is it a full flight today?'
'Could I get bumped off this flight?'
'What are the chances of me flying standby?'
'I really need to make my connection. How long is the layover in London?'

What should you say if you have to change or cancel your flight? Many people are too direct when it comes to this – just saying 'I need a new flight' is not only not professional, it makes you sound like a diva. Let's get rid of the wind machine and use some of these phrases instead.

'I'm so sorry, but I need to change/confirm my flight.'
'Could you help me change my flight, please?'
'I'm afraid I need to cancel my flight. Something's come up.'
'Is there a surcharge for this?'
'What are the next available options, please?'
'Unfortunately, due to a family emergency, I'll have to change my ticket. Could you help me, please?'

It's not always smooth sailing...oops, I mean flying. What should you say when things get turbulent? For example, what do you say midair when your tray table is broken? (Hint: 'Bring me a silver platter' is not going to cut it.) These phrases might help you feel a bit grounded (see what I did there?) during a tricky situation.

'Can someone help me with my bag?'
'I am having trouble lifting my suitcase, could you help me, please?'
'It seems that my tray table is broken.'

'I don't understand how to use the remote control.'
'May I have an extra blanket, please?'
'I would love an extra pillow – could you arrange that, please?'
'Do you have any newspapers on board? I think someone took mine.'
'It seems like my headphones aren't working – may I have another set, please?'
'I'm sorry, but I ordered a vegetarian meal.'
'It looks as though my meal is not the right one.'
'I don't understand which form I have to fill in.'
'Excuse me, would you happen to have an extra pen?'
'I'm sorry, but your seat is leaning too far back. Would you mind raising it a bit? Thank you!'
'Could you lower the sound on your headphones? I can hear everything!'
'Sorry, I'm not feeling well. Can you bring me a sick bag, please?'

NEVER CAN SAY GOODBYE

Sometimes, after certain flights, you just want to run off the plane and kiss the ground when you finally arrive at the terminal. However, it's nice to say goodbye before you go. Here are some different ways to make a grand exit. Kissing (the ground or your cabin crew) is optional.

'Thank you for a good flight!'
'Thanks for a safe flight!'
'Thank you for taking care of us — I appreciate it!'
'I'm sorry, where is the baggage claim?'
'Could you tell me the local time, please?'
'How do I get to Customs?'
'Where can I find our baggage carousel?'
'Where can I get a luggage cart?'
'Can you tell me where I transfer to my next flight?'

76. HOT WHEELS

I am sure you have a chauffered limo that takes you everywhere you need to go. But let's just say that at your next conference you have a need for speed and you want to get cruisin' down the highway and put the pedal to the metal right away.

You don't need a ticket to ride, but you do need enough vocabulary to know how to do it. Here are some helpful phrases for renting a car!

MAKING A RESERVATION

'Hi, I would like to rent a car.'
'I'm calling to find out your best rate for a Maybach from October 3rd for a week.'
'I'd like to know what your best rate is for an SUV for 10 days in September.'
'Can you let me know what cars are available in the week of August 28th?'
'Hi, I'm looking for a midsize car for the weekend of the 13th. Do you have any available?'
'I'd like to pick it up at your location but return it to another – is that possible?'
'One of the drivers is 18 years old. Is there an extra charge for this?'
'I'm looking for an automatic. Do you have any available?'
'Do all your cars have air conditioning and satellite radio?'
'Do all of your cars come with children's locks?'

BETTER TO BE SAFE THAN SORRY

Here are some phrases to use when it comes to dealing with car insurance and other exciting things. Check check!

'Do you accept foreign driver's licenses?'
'I have a Dutch driver's license – is that OK?'
'What kind of insurance do you offer?'
'Is insurance necessary?'
'Do you have a collision damage waiver?'
'What about no-risk insurance?'
'What kind of insurance would you recommend?'
'Is there an additional charge for a navigation system?'
'Is there a built-in GPS system?'
'Is there a surcharge if I bring the car back an hour late?'
'Do I have to bring it back with a full tank?'
'How much do you charge for gas?'
'Do I need to leave a deposit?'
'Can I return it to another location?'
'Are there airbags on both the driver's and the passenger's side?'
'What credit cards do you accept?'

GOT A LEMON?

Here are some phrases to use when there are problems with your car. I truly hope you never have to say any of them! But in case you do, here you go:

'I don't know where the gas tank/petrol tank is.' (Gas is American, petrol is British.)
'Can you show me how to open the trunk/boot?' (Trunk is American, boot is British – but boot is also American when it is referring to my favorite form of footwear.)
'Where is the button for the windows?'
'It seems that the brakes are not working!'
'It appears that the car's been keyed. Look at all those scratches on the side!'
'There's a huge scratch on the left door of the car.'
'The passenger seat is stained.'
'The windscreen wipers don't seem to be working.'
'I think the oil level is too low. Could you have a look?'
'I'm sorry, but there must have been a smoker in this car before me. May I have a different car, please?'
'I'm sorry, but the seatbelts seem to be defective.'

ROOM SERVICE, PLEASE

Sometimes business travel is awesome. Seeing new places and faces and bathing in claw-footed bathtubs with a glass of champagne handy is always a good thing. I want you to stay in gorgeous places and get a good deal while doing so. Just in case your personal assistant has left you for your secretary, these phrases will help you deal with hotel situations on your own. Oh, and don't steal the bathrobe. (Unless absolutely necessary.)

MAKING A RESERVATION

'Hello, I'd like to check your availability for the 19th of August, for four nights, please.'
'Hi, I'm calling for a rate check.'
'Could you tell me if you have rooms available on the 19th of August for four nights, please?'
'Hello, I'd like to make a reservation.'
'Good morning, I'd like to reserve a room.'
'I'd like a non-smoking room please, located on a quiet floor, away from the elevator/lift.'
'I'd like a room with a nice view, please.'
'Can you let me know what floors are available?'
'Do you have two adjoining rooms, by any chance?'

'What time is check in, please?'
'I'm arriving very late at night — is that a problem?'
'Do you have an airport shuttle?'
'Is there late check-out?'
'Is there a swimming pool or a fitness center?'
'What are the opening hours?'
'Do you have babysitting service?'
'Is there room service?'
'I need WiFi – do you have it in the rooms?'

LET ME SLEEP ON IT: THE BED SITUATION

'I'd like separate beds.'
'What kind of mattresses do you have?'
'Do you have a hypoallergenic mattress?'
'I'd like to know if you have a waterbed.'
'I'd like to have a king-sized bed.'
'I'd like to have a double bed.'

~ Golden Nugget of Knowledge ~

Remember that in America, a twin bed is a single bed, and a 'California king' is bigger than a king-sized bed. (It comes with a palm tree; maybe that's why.)

CH-CH-CHANGES

Now that you know all the phrases needed to make a hotel reservation, let's learn different ways to talk about changing or cancelling your reservation – as there's a chance you'll have to stay in town to go to your robot's wedding.

'I'm so sorry, but I need to change my reservation.'
'I'm afraid I have to cancel my reservation due to family circumstances.'
'It looks like my dates have changed. I'd like to change my reservation, please. Is there anything available a week later?'
'Looks like I'll be bringing a colleague with me – can we get adjoining rooms if possible?'

MY NAME IS: CHECKING IN

Let's check out different ways of checking in. (Oh, phrasal verbs, I love you.)

'Good morning, I'd like to check in, please.'
'Checking in, please.'
'What time is breakfast served?'
'I'd like to arrange a wake-up call, if that's possible.'
'Can someone help me with my bags?'
'Is there a concierge here?'
'Do you have valet parking?'
'Is there a complimentary breakfast?'
'Is there a continental breakfast?'

~ Golden Nugget of Knowledge ~

A continental breakfast is a light breakfast, usually consisting of rolls or a croissant, coffee/tea, and jam and butter. Go for the full buffet if you can!

'Do you have a map of the city, please?'
'I'm looking for a cash machine/ATM. Is there one nearby?'
'Can you recommend a good local pub/bar, please?'
'I'm interested in trying some local food. What can you recommend?'

PROBLEMS WITH…

Some of these phrases might be helpful if you find that you are staying in the Hotel from Hell. I hope you never have to say any of these!

'I'm sorry, but it seems that my key isn't working.'
'It appears that our room hasn't been cleaned.'
'It looks like the heating/air conditioning doesn't work!'
'We need a new light bulb – this one just burst!'
'We've run out of toilet paper/shampoo/soap. Could someone bring some up, please?'
'I'd like an extra/another pillow and blanket, please. These are too soft/thin/itchy/smelly!'

'We will need some extra towels. Can that be arranged?'
'I don't understand how the TV works.'
'My room faces the main street and it's very noisy. I'd like to change rooms.'
'I can hear my neighbors talking/arguing/having sex. Can I have another room immediately, please?'
'I ordered room service over 30 minutes ago, and it's still not here. How much longer do I have to wait?'
'Our tap keeps dripping. Could someone please come up and have a look at it?'
'I think the iron is broken. Can you send up a replacement, please?'
'I'd really appreciate some extra shoe polish.'
'I'm afraid my mini-bar is empty. Could someone come and refill it please?'

CHECKING OUT

When it's time to leave the building, there are many different options. Here are a few:
'I'd like to check out, please.'
'Checking out, please.'
'It looks like there were room service charges made to my room. Can I see the bill again, please?'
'It seems like there are items on the bill that we did not order.'
'I see that I've been charged for a broken lightbulb – can you explain why, please?'
'It says here that I've been charged for using the phone, but I didn't use it. Can you remove it from my bill, please?'
'What time is the next airport shuttle?'
'Could you call me a cab/taxi, please?'
'I need to get to the airport. What's the fastest way to get there?'

SAYING GOODBYE

'Thank you for your help!'
'Thank you for taking such good care of my team!'
'I'd highly recommend this hotel to my friends.'
'I'd never recommend staying here – the service was horrible!'

78. BITE ME!

Wining and dining is fun, if you're doing it with lovely people. If you'd rather put a knitting needle in your eye than have dinner with some of your colleagues, sharing a meal can be really hard work. In any case, it's important to feel confident about what to say when you're enjoying your wining and dining, or suffering through it. Here are some helpful phrases to use in a restaurant.

MAKING A RESERVATION
'Hello, I'd like to book a table for two for Saturday night.'
'Hi, are any tables available later tonight?'
'Hello, I'd like to make a reservation for a party of seven.'
'I'd like a quiet table near the window.'
'Do you have any booths available?'
'Do you have highchairs or booster seats?'
'Do you have vegetarian/vegan options?'

~ *Golden Nugget of Knowledge* ~

You might be asked, 'How many people are in your party?' Don't say, 'Oh, it's not a party. It's just a normal dinner.' (And yes, I have heard this.) 'Your party' is the number of people in your group.

BOTTOMS UP: DRINKS AT THE RESTAURANT
'Hello, may I see the wine list, please?'
'I'd like to have a look at your wine list.'
'Do you have any specialty beers?'
'I'd like to start off with a cocktail. What can you recommend?'
'What's your house wine like?'
'Can you tell me more about the local ale?'
'Cheers!'

'Bottoms up!' (Please don't confuse this with 'Up your bottom!' And yes, I have heard that. I am still recovering. And please, I beg of you, do not say 'Up yours!' when toasting someone, unless you really look good with a broken nose.)

'To your health!' (Not 'on your health'. Thank you.)

FOOD, GLORIOUS FOOD: ORDERING

'What's the special today?'

'I'd like to have the steak, medium, please. Does that come with fries?'

'What's in the house salad? Could I get a vegetarian version, please?'

'I'd like my beef to be well done, please.'

'I'm allergic to wheat. What can you recommend?'

'Is there shellfish in the soup? I don't eat shellfish.'

'I can't have any nuts or their oils due to my allergy. Could you just check with the kitchen that it's completely nut-free, please?'

'Could we have some more bread, please?'

'I dropped my fork. May I have a new one?'

'We're in a bit of a hurry. Do you know how long it will take?'

'Can that be ready within half an hour? We have tickets to the show tonight.'

'Could I substitute soy cream for the dairy cream on that?'

'I'd like a refill. Thank you!'

'Is it very spicy?'

'Can you tell me what would go well with my fish?'

'How is the trout cooked?'

'May I have a starter as a main dish?'

'Do you have a children's menu?'

'Is there an extra charge for sharing?'

. . . .

~ Golden Nugget of Knowledge ~

Please (please!) be aware that in the States a tip (gratuity) of 15% is expected, and 20% is even better. It's NOT an extra, or an afterthought, as it often is in Europe. It's actually the missing part of your server's income. Servers in America have a lower minimum wage than in other industries, and this is compensated by your generous tip. I was a waitress for many years, and we always fought over who would 'have to get' the European tourist table. Spread the news, and spread this tip! Thank you!

One more thing: If you hear or see *entrée*, this refers to your main course, not your appetizer.

· ·

WHINING AND DINING: WHAT TO SAY WHEN THINGS GO WRONG

'I'm sorry, this is not what I ordered.'
'This is burnt. Can you take it back, please?'
'We've been waiting quite a while. Can you check on our order, please?'
'Looks like you've forgotten her order – she's still waiting for her salmon!'
'I asked for extra tomatoes, not no tomatoes!'
'This fish tastes a bit off – are you sure it's fresh?'
'You brought us the wrong bill/drinks/order.'
'My glass is filthy. Please bring me another one. Thank you.'
'This is too salty – I'd like another one, please.'
'Can you bring me some extra pepper? This is too bland!'

SHOW THEM THE MONEY: WHAT TO SAY WHEN IT'S TIME TO PAY (Hey, that rhymes!)

'I'd like the check, please.'
'Could we have the bill, please?'
'I'd like to pay, thank you.'
'May I have the rest to go?'
'Do you have doggie bags?'
'I'd like to pay by credit card. Do you accept Visa?'
'Was the tip/gratuity already added to our bill?'

· ·

~ Golden Nugget of Knowledge ~

If you are dining with a large group, often a 'gratuity' will be added to your bill. This means that the tip has already been added. Usually this is about 20%.

· ·

'I'm sorry, this bill is not correct.'
'You overcharged us for our drinks. Please have a look.'
'We don't need any change, thank you.'

79. PRADA OR NADA, BABY!

Let's say your robot packed your bags. Your robot is a robot and has no sense of personal style, and is totally not aware of the latest fashion trends. You discover this, to your horror, while you are unpacking. What do you do when you need to buy new clothes (or just a gift for your favorite English coach) abroad? These phrases will make it a bit easier for you.

SHOP TILL YOU DROP
'Excuse me, do you have this in a size larger/smaller?'
'Does this come in other colors?'
'Do you have this in green?'
'Can I try this on?'
'Where is the dressing room?'
'I'm not sure what my size is. Could you measure me, please?'
'Do these run larger/smaller than normal?'
'Does this come with a matching belt?'
'Oh, I'm just looking/browsing, thank you.'
'Excuse me, do you have a men's/children's department?'
'This was the only one left on the rack. Do you have another one?'
'How much does this cost?'
'I'll take it!'
'Does this come with a case?'
'Does this come with a guarantee/warranty?'

CASH OR CREDIT?
'Excuse me, where do I pay?'
'Where is the cashier?'
'Could you call someone to help me, please?'
'Do you take credit cards?'

'Is tax included?'
'Is this on sale?'
'Is this the discounted price?'
'How long will this be on sale?'
'What is your return policy?'
'Do you give refunds?'
'Is it exchange only?'
'Is there a discount if I buy more than one?'

Problems: If you are less of a fashionista than you thought, here are some sentences to help you get back on the catwalk soon.

'I'm sorry, I need to return this.'
'This has a hole in it.'
'This ripped the first time I put it on.'
'This has a crack in it – may I have a new one, please?'
'I got this as a gift, but I already have one.'

CHAPTER 10

WHEN THE SHIT HITS THE FAN
English For Dealing With Doctors And Police

Darling reader, I want you to live a life that is full of health and happiness. And, you know, legality. However, there might be moments in your life where things may not be as good as they could be. This chapter is to help you as much as I can for when the shit hits the proverbial fan. Let's say you are abroad and get food poisoning. Or that your new iPad gets stolen on the subway. These situations suck, but not knowing how to react quickly and accurately makes it so much worse. I'll start you off with some helpful phrases to use when dealing with illness, disease, and other unwanted conditions. I'll also give you some sentences that might help you serve justice when justice needs to be served, like putting that iPad thief behind bars. And my dearest darling, I truly hope and pray that you never have to utter any of these phrases. But here they are anyway...just in case.

80. IS THERE A DOCTOR IN THE HOUSE?

'I'd like to see a doctor, please.'
'Could you call a doctor for me?'
'I need to see a doctor immediately.'
'Is there a doctor on the premises?'
'I'd like to make an appointment to see Dr Whom.'
'Do you have any doctors who speak English/Dutch/Klingon?'
'Are there any doctors who make house calls, please?'
'I'm afraid I can't get/am unable to get to the doctor's office/practice.'
'Please call an ambulance right away! He's having an attack!'
'What kind of insurance do you accept?'
'Could I get a second opinion, please?'

81. DISCUSSING SYMPTOMS: DIFFERENT WAYS TO KVETCH (GOOGLE IT!) ABOUT YOUR PROBLEMS

I've got a...
temperature.
sore throat.
headache.
lump in my arm – could you have a look at it?
swollen ankle and it's very painful to walk on.
deep cut on my thumb/toe/shin/calf/face.

I'm...
constipated.
in a lot of pain on my left side.
diabetic.
epileptic.
allergic to soy.

I have...
diarrhea.
very little energy.
severe stomach cramps.

It hurts when I...
cough.
breathe.
watch a bad Idols audition.

I'm having difficulty...
breathing.
walking.
doing the Macarena.

I might have caught...
the flu.
a stomach bug.
a cold.
a virus.

It's...
itchy.
red.
bleeding.
swollen.
shrinking.
falling off.
full of pus.

Do I need...
a bandage?
a sling?
a cast?
a splint?
a brace?
an injection?
surgery?

82. LET'S GET MEDICATED

'Could you give me a prescription for that, please?'
'I would like to know if I can drink alcohol with this medication.'
'What is the dosage?'
'Where is the nearest pharmacy?'
'When do I pick up my medication?'
'Is this a repeat prescription?'
'Is this suitable for children?'
'Where can I renew my prescription, please?'

'How long should I keep this medication?'
'Is this covered by my insurance?'
"What are the opening hours of the pharmacy?"
'How long is the antibiotic run?'
'How do you know I'm not allergic to this?'

83. YOU LOOK SO SICK! WATCH OUT FOR THE DIFFERENCES IN THESE MEANINGS

I am sick = I am ill.
I am off sick = I'm missing work because I am ill.
I feel sick = I am unwell or I feel nauseous
I'm going to be sick = I am going to vomit
I've been sick = I became ill and I'm still ill (usually used with for or since to show how long)
I was sick = I was ill but I am better now
OMG – you look so sick! = this could mean that you look unwell, or that you look really cool. My students once greeted me with this phrase and, after informing them that I was actually feeling rather great, I was happily surprised to learn that they meant I looked pretty cool that day. *insert smiley face emoticon*

JUSTICE IS BEST SERVED COLD

The next time you look at your naked wrist and realize your Apple watch is gone, I want you to take action swiftly. Let's catch that mofo and make sure it never happens again. Here we go.

84. TO CATCH A THIEF

'Help! My wallet's been stolen!'
'Someone just grabbed my iPad!'
'Hey! He took my phone!'
'Stop that man, he just took my purse!'

'Someone broke into my car!'
'My laptop is missing!'
'Call the police! It's an emergency!'
'I've been pickpocketed!'
'I saw her shoplifting!'
'There's been a robbery!'
'He tried to hold me up!'
'I've been mugged!' (Once I gave a client a new coffee mug as a gift and then I received a beautiful card that said 'Thank you for mugging me'. I love my job.)

85. AT THE POLICE STATION

'I'd like to report a theft.'
'I want to file a complaint.'
'I would like to press charges against this man.'
'I need help in finding the guy who took my bag.'
'I'd like to report a crime.'
'I've been mugged and I'd like to identify the man who did it.'
'I can describe the assailant.'
'I'd like to make a citizen's arrest. I found this woman driving drunk.'
'I would like to file a report about a noise complaint.'
'I'm the victim of a violent crime.'
'I'd like to report a hit and run.'

86. DESCRIBING THE ASSHOLE WHO DID IT

'He was tall/short/medium height.'
'She had curly/straight/wavy/blond/red/black/brown/pink/no hair.'
'He was wearing a hat/scarf/hoodie/jacket/wig/very nice pair of sparkly earrings.'
'She was working with a partner/in pairs/in a group.'
'He was fat/thin/skinny/chubby/stocky/obese/medium build.'
'He had a beard/moustache/goatee/long sideburns/tattoo/mullet/nose ring/unibrow.'

87. YOU WILL GET OVER THIS, I PROMISE YOU

'What's the next step?'
'Will you contact me with details when you know them?'
'I feel unsafe and I'd like to talk to someone.'
'Can somebody drive me home, please?'
'I'd like to keep this confidential.'
'I want to stay anonymous.'
'Please let me know when you find the bastard.'
'Is there someone I can call tomorrow if I need to?'

CHAPTER 11

ONE LANGUAGE DIVIDED BY A LOT OF WATER
The Basic Differences Between British And American English

When asked to help someone with their English, I usually ask, 'Which one would you like to learn? British? American? Australian? Indian?' There are so many dazzling possibilities to choose from! Did you know there are over 56 different accent types in the UK alone? When I coach an actor on their English film script, I always check to see which accent they need. This also applies to when I'm called in to write a press release – who is the target group and what kind of English is appropriate? It's important to get this clear when you communicate. Although the differences are not huge, they could have a huge impact if used incorrectly. Many years ago, when I was working at a prestigious language institute, a 60-year-old British colleague knocked on my door and asked, 'Can I borrow a rubber? I promise I'll give it right back when I'm done. I need it for my student. It's kind of important – we need one right now!' O.M.G. (which, at this point, stood for Order Me Gin). I was shocked, surprised, and then thought 'You GO, girl!' However, after my initial blush/admiration attack, I realized she was not actually talking about a condom, but an eraser. As it turns out, I did have one – a brand new pink one, still in its plastic wrapper. I gave it to her, and told her she could keep it for the next emergency. #truestory

PRONUNCIATION: You can't see my mouth (which is a shame, as I have a great lipstick on today) so it's a bit hard to get into here. Look online and you'll be fine. The same goes for all the vocabulary differences – there are far too many to name in this basic overview, so I have focused on the ones I felt were the most practical here. They should keep you busy for a while.

88. BASIC SPELLING DIFFERENCES

UK:
- colour, honour, labour
- centre, litre, theatre
- defence, licence, offence
- analyse, breathalyse, paralyse
- programme
- a four-storey building

US:
- color, honor, labor
- center, liter, theater
- defense, license, offense
- analyze, breathalyze, paralyze
- program
- a four-story building

89. BASIC GRAMMAR DIFFERENCES

UK:
- She burnt her finger on the stove.
- You needn't come in to work tomorrow.
- Have you got a new car?
- He hasn't got any friends.
- Shall we end the meeting early today?
- I've lost my key – can you help me find it?
- I haven't done it yet.

US:
- She burned her finger on the stove.
- You don't need to come in to work tomorrow.
- Do you have a new car?
- He doesn't have any friends.
- Should we end the meeting early today?
- I lost my key – can you help me find it?
- I didn't do it yet.

90. BASIC VOCABULARY DIFFERENCES

UK:
- ground floor, first floor, second floor
- to go on holiday
- the boot of your car
- the bonnet of your car
- the chemist's
- chips
- dustbin

US:
- first floor, second floor, third floor
- to go on vacation
- the trunk of your car
- the hood of your car
- the pharmacy/drugstore
- fries
- garbage can

UK:
- flat
- lift
- lorry
- postcode
- solicitor
- a jumper
- pants

US:
- apartment
- elevator
- truck
- zip code
- lawyer, attorney
- a sweater
- underwear

Please note: *panty* means *underwear* in English. Once a Dutch woman asked me to check if she had 'a hole in her panty'. I had to explain to her that if I did, we would be taking our relationship to a whole new level, and I would not be checking her tights. I don't know who was more embarrassed in the end. Happy to report there was no hole in her tights.

When in doubt about whether to use the British or American form, I usually advise to listen to yourself first. Do you have a more American accent? Then use American spelling and grammar. More British style? Then go with that. And remember, we will always understand you no matter which form you use, although it might lead to the occasional giggle.

CHAPTER 12

SPICE UP YOUR LIFE (AND MINE)!

100 idioms to make your life more exciting

One of the differences between good English and great English is the use of idioms. These add more color to your verbal salad and more spice to your communicative soup (which should be delicious and full of flavor, never bland). It's an effective way to make your English sound livelier. And, I promise, it will make your life, and the lives of those you are interacting with (like me!), more interesting. Now that we have nearly reached the end of our learning journey together, it's high time you got to know these idioms, which I have carefully selected just for you. I have organized them in 10 different categories to make your life a bit simpler. That's how much I love you. So, it's time to stop beating around the bush, and get the ball (which is in your court) rolling. Yes, I see what I did there.

91. SHOW ME THE MONEY

Ballpark figure – a rough estimate or approximation, usually dealing with numbers (this comes from baseball, when the announcer would look at the spectators and announce how many people were watching the game). *'How much will that new software cost? Could you give me a ballpark figure, Peter?'*

Cash cow – a business or investment that provides a steady source of income. *'That new app really proved to be quite a cash cow for Dylan!'*

Chicken feed – a ridiculously small sum of money. *'That might be chicken feed to you, but it's a month's rent to me, Ruby.'*

Deep pockets – having abundant financial resources. *'Mano's company has deep pockets – they don't mind spending money on cool launch parties.'*

Golden handcuffs – deferred payments to keep an employee from looking for work elsewhere. *'The three-year golden handcuffs will be released in April.'*

Gravy train – a situation where you can make a lot of money with little effort. *'Julia sure got on the gravy train when she sold her picture of that celebrity to that magazine!'*

Kickback – a payment made in return for facilitating a transaction. *'That political party lives on kickbacks – I don't trust them!'*

Lose your shirt –lose everything in an investment. *'Justin lost his shirt in that llama-breeding startup last year.'*

On the house – free. *'Drink up, Lindsay! The next round is on the house!'*

Put your money where your mouth is – when you take action to match your words. *'Stop saying that you want to fire him! It's time you put your money where your mouth is, Phoebe, and started doing something about it!'*

92. LET'S TALK ABOUT MARKETING AND SALES

Ahead of the curve – more advanced than the competition. *'If we continue to invest in research, I'm sure we will stay ahead of the curve, Jan.'*

Buy in bulk – to purchase large amounts of products in order to get a discount. *'Emmit wants to buy those espresso beans in bulk – can we offer him a discount?'*

Go back to square one – to start over again. *'Now that our budget has been slashed, I'm afraid we'll have to go back to square one, Tatum.'*

In the driver's seat – in control. *'The new boss was obviously not used to being in the driver's seat as he kept asking Lucas what he should be doing.'*

Keep your eye on the prize – keep focused on your main goal or reward. *'Rob, don't get worried about the competition – keep your eye on the prize and we will be fine!'*

No-brainer – something very simple or easy. *'Learning our new computer program was a real no-brainer for our tech team!'*

To come up short – to try to achieve something but fail. *'Liz wanted to raise 1 million dollars at our fundraiser, but I'm afraid we came up two thousand dollars short.'*

To get a foot in the door – to get a low-level position in the hope of getting a higher position in the future. *'Mazen got his foot in the door by working in the mailroom, but in two years he was head of the mailroom.'*

To go broke – to go bankrupt. *'The competition was too fierce and eventually they went broke.'*

To go the extra mile – to put in extra effort. *'I love working with Anneke's management team, as they always go the extra mile in meetings.'*

93. WHAT'S YOUR NUMBER?

At the eleventh hour – at the last possible moment. *'I can't believe Fern finally submitted her proposal at the eleventh hour!'*

Dressed to the nines – dressed up elegantly or smartly. *'Wow, Ivy, you are dressed to the nines! Are you off to a party?'*

First come, first served – when people are dealt with in the order of their request or arrival. *'Sorry Lew, it's first come, first serve at the cupcake counter today. Please join the line to the left!'*

Five-finger discount – shoplifting. *'Hey, that lipstick looks very expensive – did you get it with a five-finger discount, Nancy?'*

Five o'clock shadow – the stubble that appears on a man's face at the end of the day. *'I really love his five o'clock shadow, it makes him look so rugged!'*

Forty winks – a nap. *'I've got to get my forty winks in before the meeting tonight or else I won't stay awake!'*

Never in a million years – not at all likely to happen. *'I would never work for him in a million years – he is so sexist!'*

Number cruncher – a person who deals with numbers (slang). *'My accountant Laura is such a number cruncher — she's faster than a computer!'*

One-track mind – a focus on a single thought or action. *'Stop obsessing about sex! You really have a one-track mind!'*

One foot in the grave – so ill or old that death seems imminent. *'Oh, she looks terrible – it's as if she has one foot in the grave already!'*

94. TELL ME ABOUT SUCCESS AND FAILURE

The bottom fell out – When something causes a plan, project or venture to collapse or fail. *'When their design costs doubled, the bottom fell out of their kitchen renovation project.'*

Bring the house down – Give a very successful performance. *'If he sings like that on Saturday, Mari will definitely bring the house down.'*

A feather in your cap – An achievement that someone can be proud of. *'Winning that new account is a real feather in your cap, David!'*

To ace something – to do well on something. *'You are going to ace that job interview, Jeroen! You have prepared so well!'*

To cook someone's goose – To spoil that person's chances of success. *'When Charlie saw the police car arriving, she realized her goose was cooked!'*

To cut your losses – To end or withdraw from something that is already failing, in order to reduce the loss of money, time, or effort invested in it. *'That Easter Egg Graffiti project is heading for failure. Let's cut our losses before it's too late.'*

To have an ace up your sleeve – To have something in reserve that can be used to gain an advantage and obtain success. *'I'm well prepared for the negotiations. I've got an ace up my sleeve.'*

To hit pay dirt – To be lucky and suddenly find yourself in a successful money-making situation. *'Henri finally hit pay dirt with his latest invention.'*

Will never fly – will never succeed. *'A dancing school for sheep? Honey, I don't think that will ever fly.'*

With flying colors – very successfully. *'Mariette passed her entrance exam with flying colors – I'm so proud of her!'*

95. EFFICIENCY PROFICIENCY

Acid test – Proves how effective or useful something is. *'The training course was very interesting, but the acid test will come when Daniel starts his new job.'*

Leave no stone unturned – try everything possible in order to achieve or to find something. *'The management left no stone unturned in their efforts to find a solution to their personnel crisis.'*

Sail through something – succeed in doing something without much difficulty. *'Demonstrating the new product line was no problem for Yassine. He sailed through it!'*

To be on the ball – To be aware of what is happening and able to deal with things quickly and intelligently. *'We need someone who is really on the ball to head our new fund-raising campaign.'*

To fast-track something – To give something high priority so that the objective is reached as quickly as possible. *'In view of the number of homeless, it was decided to fast-track the construction of low-cost housing.'*

To get off the ground – To put something into operation after having organised it. *'After a lot of hard work, we finally got our new literacy campaign off the ground.'*

To kill two birds with one stone – To succeed in doing two things at the same time. *'By studying on the train on the way home, Bas kills two birds with one stone.'*

To take the bull by the horns – to act decisively in order to deal with a difficult situation or problem. *'Fawaz decided to take the bull by the horns and deal with his coupon-cutting addiction right away.'*

To think on your feet – To improvise. *'I'll have to think on my feet now that Finn can't do the pitch!'*

Works like a charm – When something functions very well or has the desired effect. *'Fares tested out our new app and it worked like a charm!'*

96. COLOR YOUR WORLD

The black market – illegal traffic or trade. *'Eric planned to sell those fireworks on the black market.'*

The green light – To get the go-ahead for a project. *'Bernadette just heard our team got the green light! Let's celebrate!'*

Green with envy – To be jealous or envious. *'I can't believe Rob got a new company car – I'm just green with envy!'*

In black and white – In writing. *'That proposal sounds perfect, Kareem - can I get it in black and white?'*

In the black – To be profitable or to have money in the bank. *'She has been in the black for years – I'm sure you can trust her financial advice!'*

In the red – To lose money or to be in debt with the bank. *'She could not believe that Ayham had been in the red in college – he's a millionaire now!'*

Out of the blue – All of a sudden, unexpectedly. *'Diana announced she was leaving the company out of the blue — we were shocked!'*

Red tape – Bureaucracy. *'Getting a new parking permit took Janneke months because of all the red tape!'*

To roll out the red carpet – To give someone the VIP treatment. *'I knew when they picked Amanda up from the airport in a stretch limo, they were really rolling out the red carpet!'*

A white lie – An innocent lie to not hurt someone's feelings. *'When he asked if his new skinny jeans looked good, I had to tell a white lie and say that they did.'*

97. FOOD GLORIOUS FOOD

The apple of one's eye – Someone's favorite. *'When the teacher told me my daughter was the apple of her eye, I couldn't help but hug her!'*

Baloney – Bullshit or untrue. *'I can't believe you once dated Beyoncé – that is baloney, Khalid!'*

Fishy – Unlikely or implausible; suspicious. *'I don't know about buying that used car – the whole thing seems fishy, Otto!'*

In a pickle – In a predicament or in trouble. *'Now that we have both competitors arriving at the same time, we are in quite a pickle, Angelo.'*

Lemon – A used car that breaks down too much or is of very low quality. *'Is Marijke buying a new muffler again? That car she bought on the internet is such a lemon!'*

Nuts about – Crazy about or very fond of something. *'I am just nuts about Lisa's office design – it is gorgeous!'*

Peach – A very sweet person. *'Thanks for taking me to the airport at such short notice, Tess. You are a real peach!'*

Piece of cake – Something that is easy to do. *'Putting together the new office furniture was a piece of cake – Bryon did it in an hour!'*

To cream someone – To beat someone in a (sports) competition. *'We sure got creamed in our office squash game last week!'*

To go bananas – To get really silly. *'Juliet really went bananas when she heard she won the lottery!'*

98. MAKE FRIENDS WITH ANIMALS

Bookworm – Someone who loves books and reading. *'I was such a bookworm as a child, and I still am!'*

Copycat – Someone who copies someone else. *'Stop being such a copycat – I designed that logo first!'*

Chicken – Afraid of someone or something. *'Don't be such a chicken! Just go up and ask Sylvana out!'*

Early bird – Someone who arrives or acts before the expected time. *'He's such an early bird – he's always first in line at the buffet!*

To eat like a horse – To eat a lot. *'He's so skinny and yet he eats like a horse!'*

To make an ass of yourself – To be an embarrassment to yourself. *'I'm sorry I started dancing on the table during the office party. I must have made a real ass out of myself.'*

Pigheaded – Someone who is stubborn or not flexible. *'He was too pig-headed to listen to our new ideas.'*

To smell a rat – To mistrust a situation. *'I wonder why their office closed so suddenly. I smell a rat!*

To talk turkey – To talk honestly. *'Can we talk turkey here? I really don't like your adapted proposal.'*

To work like a dog – To work very hard. *'I hope my boss likes Amer's outline – he really worked like a dog on it!'*

99. WHERE IT'S AT

Dirt cheap – Very cheap. *'Daphne was able to buy that painting dirt cheap at an auction last week!'*

Down to earth – Unpretentious. *'She is so down to earth – I thought she would be arrogant, but she's not at all!'*

Once in a blue moon – Once in a long while. *'Once in a blue moon we'll order sushi for lunch.'*

Out of this world – Incredible or extraordinary. *'Wow, that launch was really out of this world – it was incredible that they had real tigers!'*

Over the hill – Too old. *'He must be getting over the hill – he's so out of breath after he goes up the stairs.'*

The tip of the iceberg – A small part of a much larger problem or situation. *'That missing 100 euros is just the tip of the iceberg, I'm afraid. We'll have to check all our books, Gaston!'*

To go downhill – When a situation gets bad or worse. *'Our sales have really gone downhill since we changed our company name to Dead Puppies International.'*

To make a mountain out of a molehill – To make a big deal out of something that's not important. *'Stop complaining about the color of the new paperclips, Laura – you are really making a mountain out of a molehill!'*

To win by a landslide – to win by a large majority. *'Priya's recycling campaign won by a landslide!'*

Up the creek – In trouble. *'We are really up the creek on this one, Liedewij – I can't believe our computer was hacked!'*

100. HE SHOOTS, HE SCORES

Blindsided – To not see something coming. *'Rikke was totally blindsided when they gave the new job to Jop.'*

Call the shots – Make the decisions. *'Nol made it pretty clear that he was calling the shots when he vetoed the new proposal.'*

Down to the wire – Right at the very end. *'It's coming down to the wire to get this completed before the deadline.'*

The front runner – The person in the lead or who is expected to win. *'Saskia is the front runner for the new barista position.'*

Get a second wind – Get renewed energy. *'Carine got her second wind around 11 P.M. and worked through the night!'*

Go to bat for someone – Defend someone. *'Thanks for going to the bat for me in the meeting, Raffaela – I really appreciate it!'*

Hit below the belt – Do or say something that is unfair. *'Michel, that's really below the belt to judge her based on her appearance.'*

Keep your head above water – Keep up with your work or responsibilities. *'Anouk really has to keep her head above water juggling all those new projects!'*

No sweat – Don't worry. *'You need this done by lunchtime? No sweat, Mieke will take care of it right away.'*

To learn the ropes – to understand new things. *'The first week on the job you'll be learning the ropes from Paul.'*

My darling, YOU HAVE COMPLETED YOUR LEARNING JOURNEY!

Thank you so much for sticking with me and working so hard on improving your communication skills. I hope you now feel ready to rock when it comes to professional English! How's your ass? Does it feel saved? It should!

Well done!

ACKNOWLEDGMENTS

AN ATTITUDE OF GRATITUDE

What you are holding in your hands is the product of Buffiland. I live there a lot when I'm writing. (Also when I'm not writing.) Buffiland is a compact yet complex metropolis. It has sushi growing on trees and gin-and-tonic waterfalls. Concepts such as negativity, violence, and calories are gently trampled by glitter-shod unicorns. But the most amazing thing about Buffiland is the people who live there. I'd like to thank them here, as they contributed to the creation and completion of this book.

Thank you to my family, my friends, my clients, and my students. You all inspire me every day to dream bigger, do better, and think harder. I cannot thank you enough for your comfort, your love, your offers of alcohol, chocolate, and caffeine (which I gleefully accepted by the bucketful), your spontaneous hugs, your semisexy photos of sumo wrestlers that were texted to me at just the right time, the perfectly chosen emoticons that filled my screen daily (this means you, Anneke), and your unwavering support of me and my dreams. This book holds many hearts. It holds yours.

A Super Special Shout Out to my friends who I've had the honor of teaching at the emergency tent camp in Rosmalen. You are all so brave, so kind, and so wise. You've taught me more than I could ever teach you. I hope that this book in some small way can help you have a better life here in the Netherlands. I'm so blessed to have you as my friends and I love you. Now go study your Dutch verbs.

A Very Special Thank You to my team who helped me with the Nitty Gritty Nuts and Bolts Hard Work part of this book. You kept me sane, happy, and organized. And how you did this all legally is beyond me, but I'm so grateful you did. Nancy Poleon of Branded Personalities, thank you for managing me and this project – so often you were the voice of reason. Juliet Jonkers, thank for being the best editor/ cheerleader a girl could ever hope for – you always knew what to say and exactly how to say it. Peter Kortleve, you get me so well and that comes through beautifully in your creations. Thank you for designing this book inside and out and taking it to another level. Lidewijde Paris, thank you for letting me pick your brain while stealing your shrimp. Your advice was gold, just like your heart. Laura Magzis, I'm so glad I could get you in on this one as a coronation of nearly 30 years of friendship. I loved your quibbles at least 3 times. Sweet Jeroen Konings, thank you for your eagle eyes and the mullet. Thank you, sweet Jan Marijnissen for the foreword to this book. I treasure our friendship – may it continue for years to come. Ringel Goslinga, thank you for letting me use your fantastic photo from the NRC on the back cover; I am honored. Thank you to Rijnske Koelewijn, Caro Emerald, and Merijn Everaarts for your kind words on the back of this book. I am humbled.

And a huge Duberman Death Grip Hug for each and every one of the crowdfunders of this book. Without your generous support, this book would never have made it into your hands. Thank you all for your trust. I jumped, and you caught me. And how! I would also like to thank you on behalf of the 100+ refugees who got a free book and will continue to benefit from book sales in the future. Deep bow to all of you (after I'm done hugging you).

A 'THERE ARE NO WORDS TO EXPRESS HOW I FEEL SO I WILL JUST SAY ASLFANAGAFD' THANK YOU to Ruby Luna and Dylan Sol. Let me reintroduce myself to you both. Hi. I'm your mom, and I gave you life. (I love how that line works when I ask you to bring me wine when I'm flopped on the couch.) You are the best former residents I could ever ask for, and you make me laugh every single day. I love you so much and am so proud to be your mama. You were with me in every word in this book, as you are the driving force behind all of them. Now that this book is done, I promise I will get my own wine from now on.

And the simplest Thank You of all goes to my hubby/ex-boyfriend Peter, my rock since the moment we locked eyes in 1990. (OK, it was in the middle of the night and I was squinting, but still.) I know life with me isn't always easy, normal, or predictable. Thank God you never want to be bored. You have changed my life in a million marvelous ways, like helping me give birth to two people and three books so far. (You also played a pretty important role in their conception.)

My dearest darling, you are the mayor of Buffiland.

I love you more than stars and sand
I trace your lines inside my hand.

All of you have made feeling *grateful* feel so *great* and so *full*. Thank you.

Buffi Duberman

APRIL, 2016

You did it!